D1089598

FREE Test Taking Tips DVD Offer

To help us better serve you, we have developed a Test Taking Tips DVD that we would like to give you for FREE. **This DVD covers world-class test taking tips that you can use to be even more successful when you are taking your test.**

All that we ask is that you email us your feedback about your study guide. Please let us know what you thought about it – whether that is good, bad or indifferent.

To get your **FREE Test Taking Tips DVD**, email freedvd@studyguideteam.com with "FREE DVD" in the subject line and the following information in the body of the email:

    a. The title of your study guide.

    b. Your product rating on a scale of 1-5, with 5 being the highest rating.

    c. Your feedback about the study guide. What did you think of it?

    d. Your full name and shipping address to send your free DVD.

If you have any questions or concerns, please don't hesitate to contact us at freedvd@studyguideteam.com.

Thanks again!

Correction Officer Exam Study Guide

Correctional Officer Test Prep Team

Table of Contents

Quick Overview

As you draw closer to taking your exam, effective preparation becomes more and more important. Thankfully, you have this study guide to help you get ready. Use this guide to help keep your studying on track and refer to it often.

This study guide contains several key sections that will help you be successful on your exam. The guide contains tips for what you should do the night before and the day of the test. Also included are test-taking tips. Knowing the right information is not always enough. Many well-prepared test takers struggle with exams. These tips will help equip you to accurately read, assess, and answer test questions.

A large part of the guide is devoted to showing you what content to expect on the exam and to helping you better understand that content. Near the end of this guide is a practice test so that you can see how well you have grasped the content. Then, answer explanations are provided so that you can understand why you missed certain questions.

Don't try to cram the night before you take your exam. This is not a wise strategy for a few reasons. First, your retention of the information will be low. Your time would be better used by reviewing information you already know rather than trying to learn a lot of new information. Second, you will likely become stressed as you try to gain a large amount of knowledge in a short amount of time. Third, you will be depriving yourself of sleep. So be sure to go to bed at a reasonable time the night before. Being well-rested helps you focus and remain calm.

Be sure to eat a substantial breakfast the morning of the exam. If you are taking the exam in the afternoon, be sure to have a good lunch as well. Being hungry is distracting and can make it difficult to focus. You have hopefully spent lots of time preparing for the exam. Don't let an empty stomach get in the way of success!

When travelling to the testing center, leave earlier than needed. That way, you have a buffer in case you experience any delays. This will help you remain calm and will keep you from missing your appointment time at the testing center.

Be sure to pace yourself during the exam. Don't try to rush through the exam. There is no need to risk performing poorly on the exam just so you can leave the testing center early. Allow yourself to use all of the allotted time if needed.

Remain positive while taking the exam even if you feel like you are performing poorly. Thinking about the content you should have mastered will not help you perform better on the exam.

Once the exam is complete, take some time to relax. Even if you feel that you need to take the exam again, you will be well served by some down time before you begin studying again. It's often easier to convince yourself to study if you know that it will come with a reward!

Test-Taking Strategies

1. Predicting the Answer

When you feel confident in your preparation for a multiple-choice test, try predicting the answer before reading the answer choices. This is especially useful on questions that test objective factual knowledge or that ask you to fill in a blank. By predicting the answer before reading the available choices, you eliminate the possibility that you will be distracted or led astray by an incorrect answer choice. You will feel more confident in your selection if you read the question, predict the answer, and then find your prediction among the answer choices. After using this strategy, be sure to still read all of the answer choices carefully and completely. If you feel unprepared, you should not attempt to predict the answers. This would be a waste of time and an opportunity for your mind to wander in the wrong direction.

2. Reading the Whole Question

Too often, test takers scan a multiple-choice question, recognize a few familiar words, and immediately jump to the answer choices. Test authors are aware of this common impatience, and they will sometimes prey upon it. For instance, a test author might subtly turn the question into a negative, or he or she might redirect the focus of the question right at the end. The only way to avoid falling into these traps is to read the entirety of the question carefully before reading the answer choices.

3. Looking for Wrong Answers

Long and complicated multiple-choice questions can be intimidating. One way to simplify a difficult multiple-choice question is to eliminate all of the answer choices that are clearly wrong. In most sets of answers, there will be at least one selection that can be dismissed right away. If the test is administered on paper, the test taker could draw a line through it to indicate that it may be ignored; otherwise, the test taker will have to perform this operation mentally or on scratch paper. In either case, once the obviously incorrect answers have been eliminated, the remaining choices may be considered. Sometimes identifying the clearly wrong answers will give the test taker some information about the correct answer. For instance, if one of the remaining answer choices is a direct opposite of one of the eliminated answer choices, it may well be the correct answer. The opposite of obviously wrong is obviously right! Of course, this is not always the case. Some answers are obviously incorrect simply because they are irrelevant to the question being asked. Still, identifying and eliminating some incorrect answer choices is a good way to simplify a multiple-choice question.

4. Don't Overanalyze

Anxious test takers often overanalyze questions. When you are nervous, your brain will often run wild, causing you to make associations and discover clues that don't actually exist. If you feel that this may be a problem for you, do whatever you can to slow down during the test. Try taking a deep breath or counting to ten. As you read and consider the question, restrict yourself to the particular words used by the author. Avoid thought tangents about what the author *really* meant, or what he or she was *trying* to say. The only things that matter on a multiple-choice test are the words that are actually in the question. You must avoid reading too much into a multiple-choice question, or supposing that the writer meant something other than what he or she wrote.

5. No Need for Panic

It is wise to learn as many strategies as possible before taking a multiple-choice test, but it is likely that you will come across a few questions for which you simply don't know the answer. In this situation, avoid panicking. Because most multiple-choice tests include dozens of questions, the relative value of a single wrong answer is small. Moreover, your failure on one question has no effect on your success elsewhere on the test. As much as possible, you should compartmentalize each question on a multiple-choice test. In other words, you should not allow your feelings about one question to affect your success on the others. When you find a question that you either don't understand or don't know how to answer, just take a deep breath and do your best. Read the entire question slowly and carefully. Try rephrasing the question a couple of different ways. Then, read all of the answer choices carefully. After eliminating obviously wrong answers, make a selection and move on to the next question.

6. Confusing Answer Choices

When working on a difficult multiple-choice question, there may be a tendency to focus on the answer choices that are the easiest to understand. Many people, whether consciously or not, gravitate to the answer choices that require the least concentration, knowledge, and memory. This is a mistake. When you come across an answer choice that is confusing, you should give it extra attention. A question might be confusing because you do not know the subject matter to which it refers. If this is the case, don't eliminate the answer before you have affirmatively settled on another. When you come across an answer choice of this type, set it aside as you look at the remaining choices. If you can confidently assert that one of the other choices is correct, you can leave the confusing answer aside. Otherwise, you will need to take a moment to try to better understand the confusing answer choice. Rephrasing is one way to tease out the sense of a confusing answer choice.

7. Your First Instinct

Many people struggle with multiple-choice tests because they overthink the questions. If you have studied sufficiently for the test, you should be prepared to trust your first instinct once you have carefully and completely read the question and all of the answer choices. There is a great deal of research suggesting that the mind can come to the correct conclusion very quickly once it has obtained all of the relevant information. At times, it may seem to you as if your intuition is working faster even than your reasoning mind. This may in fact be true. The knowledge you obtain while studying may be retrieved from your subconscious before you have a chance to work out the associations that support it. Verify your instinct by working out the reasons that it should be trusted.

8. Key Words

Many test takers struggle with multiple-choice questions because they have poor reading comprehension skills. Quickly reading and understanding a multiple-choice question requires a mixture of skill and experience. To help with this, try jotting down a few key words and phrases on a piece of scrap paper. Doing this concentrates the process of reading and forces the mind to weigh the relative importance of the question's parts. In selecting words and phrases to write down, the test taker thinks about the question more deeply and carefully. This is especially true for multiple-choice questions that are preceded by a long prompt.

9. Subtle Negatives

One of the oldest tricks in the multiple-choice test writer's book is to subtly reverse the meaning of a question with a word like *not* or *except*. If you are not paying attention to each word in the question, you can easily be led astray by this trick. For instance, a common question format is, "Which of the following is…?" Obviously, if the question instead is, "Which of the following is not…?," then the answer will be quite different. Even worse, the test makers are aware of the potential for this mistake and will include one answer choice that would be correct if the question were not negated or reversed. A test taker who misses the reversal will find what he or she believes to be a correct answer and will be so confident that he or she will fail to reread the question and discover the original error. The only way to avoid this is to practice a wide variety of multiple-choice questions and to pay close attention to each and every word.

10. Reading Every Answer Choice

It may seem obvious, but you should always read every one of the answer choices! Too many test takers fall into the habit of scanning the question and assuming that they understand the question because they recognize a few key words. From there, they pick the first answer choice that answers the question they believe they have read. Test takers who read all of the answer choices might discover that one of the latter answer choices is actually *more* correct. Moreover, reading all of the answer choices can remind you of facts related to the question that can help you arrive at the correct answer. Sometimes, a misstatement or incorrect detail in one of the latter answer choices will trigger your memory of the subject and will enable you to find the right answer. Failing to read all of the answer choices is like not reading all of the items on a restaurant menu: you might miss out on the perfect choice.

11. Spot the Hedges

One of the keys to success on multiple-choice tests is paying close attention to every word. This is never more true than with words like *almost*, *most*, *some*, and *sometimes*. These words are called "hedges" because they indicate that a statement is not totally true or not true in every place and time. An absolute statement will contain no hedges, but in many subjects, like literature and history, the answers are not always straightforward or absolute. There are always exceptions to the rules in these subjects. For this reason, you should favor those multiple-choice questions that contain hedging language. The presence of qualifying words indicates that the author is taking special care with his or her words, which is certainly important when composing the right answer. After all, there are many ways to be wrong, but there is only one way to be right! For this reason, it is wise to avoid answers that are absolute when taking a multiple-choice test. An absolute answer is one that says things are either all one way or all another. They often include words like *every*, *always*, *best*, and *never*. If you are taking a multiple-choice test in a subject that doesn't lend itself to absolute answers, be on your guard if you see any of these words.

12. Long Answers

In many subject areas, the answers are not simple. As already mentioned, the right answer often requires hedges. Another common feature of the answers to a complex or subjective question are qualifying clauses, which are groups of words that subtly modify the meaning of the sentence. If the question or answer choice describes a rule to which there are exceptions or the subject matter is complicated, ambiguous, or confusing, the correct answer will require many words in order to be expressed clearly and accurately. In essence, you should not be deterred by answer choices that seem excessively long. Oftentimes, the author of the text will not be able to write the correct answer without offering some qualifications and modifications. Your job is to read the answer choices thoroughly and completely and to select the one that most accurately and precisely answers the question.

13. Restating to Understand

Sometimes, a question on a multiple-choice test is difficult not because of what it asks but because of how it is written. If this is the case, restate the question or answer choice in different words. This process serves a couple of important purposes. First, it forces you to concentrate on the core of the question. In order to rephrase the question accurately, you have to understand it well. Rephrasing the question will concentrate your mind on the key words and ideas. Second, it will present the information to your mind in a fresh way. This process may trigger your memory and render some useful scrap of information picked up while studying.

14. True Statements

Sometimes an answer choice will be true in itself, but it does not answer the question. This is one of the main reasons why it is essential to read the question carefully and completely before proceeding to the answer choices. Too often, test takers skip ahead to the answer choices and look for true statements. Having found one of these, they are content to select it without reference to the question above. Obviously, this provides an easy way for test makers to play tricks. The savvy test taker will always read the entire question before turning to the answer choices. Then, having settled on a correct answer choice, he or she will refer to the original question and ensure that the selected answer is relevant. The mistake of choosing a correct-but-irrelevant answer choice is especially common on questions related to specific pieces of objective knowledge, like historical or scientific facts. A prepared test taker will have a wealth of factual knowledge at his or her disposal, and should not be careless in its application.

15. No Patterns

One of the more dangerous ideas that circulates about multiple-choice tests is that the correct answers tend to fall into patterns. These erroneous ideas range from a belief that B and C are the most common right answers, to the idea that an unprepared test-taker should answer "A-B-A-C-A-D-A-B-A." It cannot be emphasized enough that pattern-seeking of this type is exactly the WRONG way to approach a multiple-choice test. To begin with, it is highly unlikely that the test maker will plot the correct answers according to some predetermined pattern. The questions are scrambled and delivered in a random order. Furthermore, even if the test maker was following a pattern in the assignation of correct answers, there is no reason why the test taker would know which pattern he or she was using. Any attempt to discern a pattern in the answer choices is a waste of time and a distraction from the real work of taking the test. A test taker would be much better served by extra preparation before the test than by reliance on a pattern in the answers.

FREE DVD OFFER

Don't forget that doing well on your exam includes both understanding the test content and understanding how to use what you know to do well on the test. We offer a completely FREE Test Taking Tips DVD that covers world class test taking tips that you can use to be even more successful when you are taking your test.

All that we ask is that you email us your feedback about your study guide. To get your **FREE Test Taking Tips DVD**, email freedvd@studyguideteam.com with "FREE DVD" in the subject line and the following information in the body of the email:

- The title of your study guide.
- Your product rating on a scale of 1-5, with 5 being the highest rating.
- Your feedback about the study guide. What did you think of it?
- Your full name and shipping address to send your free DVD.

Introduction

Function of the Test

Persons seeking employment as a corrections officer in the United States must typically take and pass an exam to demonstrate readiness and/or aptitude for employment in the corrections field. Some states have dedicated exams that are to be used only in that state. Others provide exams that are used by corrections departments in various states nationwide. Still others provide generic skills or placement tests used by colleges and other non-corrections programs. In all cases, states and state corrections employers look for prospective employees to reach a minimum passing score before they will be considered.

In most cases, individuals taking a corrections exam are younger individuals beginning their careers, or individuals looking to move from a field such as the military or policing and go into corrections. Tests are administered during the hiring process, and test scores are rarely used for any purpose other than ensuring that applicants meet a set minimum level of readiness for the profession.

Test Administration

Details of where, when, and how often corrections exams are administered vary from state-to-state. Some states use in-house testing procedures, while many outsource their corrections exams to third-party testing centers. States typically do permit retesting for test-takers who do not pass a corrections exam on their first attempt, although some states place limits on retesting. For example, some permit a limited number of retest attempts or require that test-takers wait a certain amount of time before attempting the test again.

All states are required to make accommodations for test-takers with disabilities in keeping with the Americans with Disabilities Act. This typically means that a test-taker with a documented disability can receive accommodations such as additional time or specialized printed material for an exam. Test-takers requiring accommodations should contact potential employers prior to registering for the exam.

Test Format

The format of a corrections exam varies from state to state, but usually involves testing of general reading, writing, and mathematical skills, as well as testing of skills more specific to job duties as a corrections officer. For example, in Texas, candidates take a pre-employment test consisting of 100 questions in five parts: Memory and Observation, Situational Reasoning, Reading Comprehension/Deductive Reasoning, Verbal Reasoning, and Arithmetic. In Massachusetts, candidates face 80 multiple-choice questions covering six abilities: the ability to gather information, the ability to write concisely and accurately, the ability to read, understand, explain, and apply information, the ability to work accurately with names, numbers, codes and/or symbols, the ability to analyze and determine the applicability of quantitative and qualitative data, and the ability to maintain accurate records. In Georgia, candidates are simply required to take either the ASSET or COMPASS tests—two general college placement exams covering language and mathematical skills.

Scoring

Scoring methods and requirements also vary from state to state, with most states requiring scores comparable to those obtained by students being placed into beginning community college courses. States tend to have slightly higher requirements for scores on language sections than on mathematical and other sections of corrections exams.

Recent/Future Developments

States are regularly changing the tests they require, so interested applicants should check with their state or their prospective employer for the latest information about changes.

Reading Comprehension

Literary Analysis

The Purpose of a Passage

When it comes to an author's writing, readers should always identify a position or stance. No matter how objective a text may seem, readers should assume the author has preconceived beliefs. One can reduce the likelihood of accepting an invalid argument by looking for multiple articles on the topic, including those with varying opinions. If several opinions point in the same direction and are backed by reputable peer-reviewed sources, it's more likely the author has a valid argument. Positions that run contrary to widely held beliefs and existing data should invite scrutiny. There are exceptions to the rule, so be a careful consumer of information.

Though themes, symbols, and motifs are buried deep within the text and can sometimes be difficult to infer, an author's purpose is usually obvious from the beginning. No matter the genre or format, all authors are writing to persuade, inform, entertain, or express feelings. Often, these purposes are blended, with one dominating the rest. It's useful to learn to recognize the author's intent.

Persuasive writing is used to persuade or convince readers of something. It often contains two elements: the argument and the counterargument. The argument takes a stance on an issue, while the counterargument pokes holes in the opposition's stance. Authors rely on logic, emotion, and writer credibility to persuade readers to agree with them. If readers are opposed to the stance before reading, they are unlikely to adopt that stance. However, those who are undecided or committed to the same stance are more likely to agree with the author.

Informative writing tries to teach or inform. Workplace manuals, instructor lessons, statistical reports and cookbooks are examples of informative texts. Informative writing is usually based on facts and is often void of emotion and persuasion. Informative texts generally contain statistics, charts, and graphs. Though most informative texts lack a persuasive agenda, readers must examine the text carefully to determine whether one exists within a given passage.

Stories or narratives are designed to entertain. When you go to the movies, you often want to escape for a few hours, not necessarily to think critically. Entertaining writing is designed to delight and engage the reader. However, sometimes this type of writing can be woven into more serious materials, such as persuasive or informative writing to hook the reader before transitioning into a more scholarly discussion.

Emotional writing works to evoke the reader's feelings, such as anger, euphoria, or sadness. The connection between reader and author is an attempt to cause the reader to share the author's intended emotion or tone. Sometimes in order to make a piece more poignant, the author simply wants readers to feel emotion that the author has felt. Other times, the author attempts to persuade or manipulate the reader into adopting his stance. While it's okay to sympathize with the author, be aware of the individual's underlying intent.

The various writing styles are usually blended, with one purpose dominating the rest. A persuasive text, for example, might begin with a humorous tale to make readers more receptive to the persuasive message, or a recipe in a cookbook designed to inform might be preceded by an entertaining anecdote that makes the recipes more appealing.

Identify Passage Characteristics

Writing can be classified under four passage types: narrative, expository, technical, and persuasive. Though these types are not mutually exclusive, one form tends to dominate the rest. By recognizing the *type* of passage you're reading, you gain insight into *how* you should read. When reading a narrative intended to entertain, sometimes you can read more quickly through the passage if the details are discernible. A technical document, on the other hand, might require a close read, because skimming the passage might cause the reader to miss salient details.

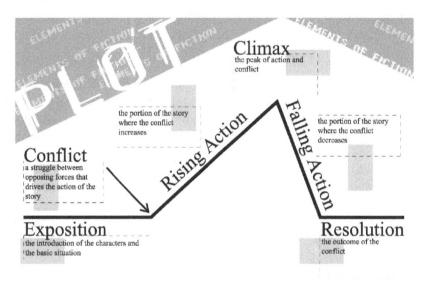

1. Narrative writing, at its core, is the art of storytelling. For a narrative to exist, certain elements must be present. It must have characters. While many characters are human, characters could be defined as anything that thinks, acts, and talks like a human. For example, many recent movies, such as *Lord of the Rings* and *The Chronicles of Narnia*, include animals, fantasty creatures, and even trees that behave like humans. Narratives also must have a plot or sequence of events. Typically, those events follow a standard plot diagram, but recent trends start *in medias res* or in the middle (nearer the climax). In this instance, foreshadowing and flashbacks often fill in plot details. Along with characters and a plot, there must also be conflict. Conflict is usually divided into two types: internal and external. Internal conflict indicates the character is in turmoil. Think of an angel on one shoulder and the devil on the other, arguing it out. Internal conflicts are presented through the character's thoughts. External conflicts are visible. Types of external conflict include person versus person, person versus nature, person versus technology, person versus the supernatural, or a person versus fate.

2. Expository writing is detached and to the point, while other types of writing — persuasive, narrative, and descriptive — are livelier. Since expository writing is designed to instruct or inform, it usually involves directions and steps written in second person ("you" voice) and lacks any persuasive or narrative elements. Sequence words such as *first*, *second*, and *third*, or *in the first place*, *secondly*, and *lastly* are often given to add fluency and cohesion. Common examples of expository writing include instructor's lessons, cookbook recipes, and repair manuals.

3. Due to its empirical nature, technical writing is filled with steps, charts, graphs, data, and statistics. The goal of technical writing is to advance understanding in a field through the scientific method. Experts such as teachers, doctors, or mechanics use words unique to the profession in which they operate. These words, which often incorporate acronyms, are called *jargon*. Technical writing is a type of expository writing, but is not meant to be understood by the general public. Instead, technical writers assume readers have received a formal education in a particular field of study and need no explanation as to what the jargon means. Imagine a doctor trying to understand a diagnostic reading for a car or a mechanic trying to interpret lab results. Only professionals with proper training will fully comprehend the text.

4. Persuasive writing is designed to change opinions and attitudes. The topic, stance, and arguments are found in the thesis, positioned near the end of the introduction. Later supporting paragraphs offer relevant quotations, paraphrases, and summaries from primary or secondary sources, which are then interpreted, analyzed, and evaluated. The goal of persuasive writers is not to stack quotes, but to develop original ideas by using sources as a starting point. Good persuasive writing makes powerful arguments with valid sources and thoughtful analysis. Poor persuasive writing is riddled with bias and logical fallacies. Sometimes, logical and illogical arguments are sandwiched together in the same text. Therefore, readers should display skepticism when reading persuasive arguments.

Text Structure

Depending on what the author is attempting to accomplish, certain formats or text structures work better than others. For example, a sequence structure might work for narration but not when identifying similarities and differences between dissimilar concepts. Similarly, a comparison-contrast structure is not useful for narration. It's the author's job to put the right information in the correct format.

Readers should be familiar with the five main literary structures:

1. *Sequence* structure (sometimes referred to as the order structure) is when the order of events proceed in a predictable order. In many cases, this means the text goes through the plot elements: exposition, rising action, climax, falling action, and resolution. Readers are introduced to characters, setting, and conflict in the exposition. In the rising action, there's an increase in tension and suspense. The climax is the height of tension and the point of no return. Tension decreases during the falling action. In the resolution, any conflicts presented in the exposition are solved, and the story concludes. An informative text that is structured sequentially will often go in order from one step to the next.

2. In the *problem-solution* structure, authors identify a potential problem and suggest a solution. This form of writing is usually divided into two paragraphs and can be found in informational texts. For example, cell phone, cable and satellite providers use this structure in manuals to help customers troubleshoot or identify problems with services or products.

3. When authors want to discuss similarities and differences between separate concepts, they arrange thoughts in a *comparison-contrast* paragraph structure. Venn diagrams are an effective graphic organizer for comparison-contrast structures, because they feature two overlapping circles that can be used to organize similarities and differences. A comparison-contrast essay organizes one paragraph based on similarities and another based on differences. A comparison-contrast essay can also be

arranged with the similarities and differences of individual traits addressed within individual paragraphs. Words such as *however*, *but*, and *nevertheless* help signal a contrast in ideas.

4. *Descriptive* writing structure is designed to appeal to your senses. Much like an artist who constructs a painting, good descriptive writing builds an image in the reader's mind by appealing to the five senses: sight, hearing, taste, touch, and smell. However, overly descriptive writing can become tedious; sparse descriptions can make settings and characters seem flat. Good authors strike a balance by applying descriptions only to passages, characters, and settings that are integral to the plot.

5. Passages that use the *cause and effect* structure are simply asking *why* by demonstrating some type of connection between ideas. Words such as *if*, *since*, *because*, *then*, or *consequently* indicate relationship. By switching the order of a complex sentence, the writer can rearrange the emphasis on different clauses. Saying *If Sheryl is late, we'll miss the dance* is different from saying *We'll miss the dance if Sheryl is late*. One emphasizes Sheryl's tardiness while the other emphasizes missing the dance. Paragraphs can also be arranged in a cause and effect format. Since the format — before and after — is sequential, it is useful when authors wish to discuss the impact of choices. Researchers often apply this paragraph structure to the scientific method.

Point of View

Point of view is an important writing device to consider. In fiction writing, point of view refers to who tells the story or from whose perspective readers are observing as they read. In non-fiction writing, the *point of view* refers to whether the author refers to himself/herself, his/her readers, or chooses not to refer to either. Whether fiction or nonfiction, the author will carefully consider the impact the perspective will have on the purpose and main point of the writing.

- *First-person point of view*: The story is told from the writer's perspective. In fiction, this would mean that the main character is also the narrator. First-person point of view is easily recognized by the use of personal pronouns such as *I*, *me*, *we*, *us*, *our*, *my*, and *myself*.

- *Third-person point of view*: In a more formal essay, this would be an appropriate perspective because the focus should be on the subject matter, not the writer or the reader. Third-person point of view is recognized by the use of the pronouns *he*, *she*, *they*, and *it*. In fiction writing, third person point of view has a few variations.

  o *Third-person limited* point of view refers to a story told by a narrator who has access to the thoughts and feelings of just one character.

  o In *third-person omniscient* point of view, the narrator has access to the thoughts and feelings of all the characters.

  o In *third-person objective* point of view, the narrator is like a fly on the wall and can see and hear what the characters do and say, but does not have access to their thoughts and feelings.

- *Second-person point of view*: This point of view isn't commonly used in fiction or non-fiction writing because it directly addresses the reader using the pronouns *you*, *your*, and *yourself*. Second-person perspective is more appropriate in direct communication, such as business letters or emails.

Point of View	Pronouns Used
First person	I, me, we, us, our, my, myself
Second person	You, your, yourself
Third person	He, she, it, they

Style, Tone, and Mood

Style, tone, and mood are often thought to be the same thing. Though they're closely related, there are important differences to keep in mind. The easiest way to do this is to remember that style "creates and affects" tone and mood. More specifically, style is how the writer uses words to create the desired tone and mood for their writing.

Style
Style can include any number of technical writing choices. A few examples of style choices include:

- Sentence Construction: When presenting facts, does the writer use shorter sentences to create a quicker sense of the supporting evidence, or do they use longer sentences to elaborate and explain the information?

- Technical Language: Does the writer use jargon to demonstrate their expertise in the subject, or do they use ordinary language to help the reader understand things in simple terms?

- Formal Language: Does the writer refrain from using contractions such as won't or can't to create a more formal tone, or do they use a colloquial, conversational style to connect to the reader?

- Formatting: Does the writer use a series of shorter paragraphs to help the reader follow a line of argument, or do they use longer paragraphs to examine an issue in great detail and demonstrate their knowledge of the topic?

On the test, examine the writer's style and how their writing choices affect the way the text comes across.

Tone
Tone refers to the writer's attitude toward the subject matter. Tone is usually explained in terms of a work of fiction. For example, the tone conveys how the writer feels about their characters and the situations in which they're involved. Nonfiction writing is sometimes thought to have no tone at all; however, this is incorrect.

A lot of nonfiction writing has a neutral tone, which is an important tone for the writer to take. A neutral tone demonstrates that the writer is presenting a topic impartially and letting the information speak for itself. On the other hand, nonfiction writing can be just as effective and appropriate if the tone isn't neutral. For instance, take this example involving seat belts:

> Seat belts save more lives than any other automobile safety feature. Many studies show that airbags save lives as well; however, not all cars have airbags. For instance, some older cars don't. Furthermore, air bags aren't entirely reliable. For example, studies show that in 15% of accidents airbags don't deploy as designed, but, on the other hand, seat belt malfunctions are extremely rare. The number of highway fatalities has plummeted since laws requiring seat belt usage were enacted.

In this passage, the writer mostly chooses to retain a neutral tone when presenting information. If the writer would instead include their own personal experience of losing a friend or family member in a car accident, the tone would change dramatically. The tone would no longer be neutral and would show that the writer has a personal stake in the content, allowing them to interpret the information in a different way. When analyzing tone, consider what the writer is trying to achieve in the text and how they *create* the tone using style.

Mood
Mood refers to the feelings and atmosphere that the writer's words create for the reader. Like tone, many nonfiction texts can have a neutral mood. To return to the previous example, if the writer would choose to include information about a person they know being killed in a car accident, the text would suddenly carry an emotional component that is absent in the previous example. Depending on how they present the information, the writer can create a sad, angry, or even hopeful mood. When analyzing the mood, consider what the writer wants to accomplish and whether the best choice was made to achieve that end.

Consistency

Whatever style, tone, and mood the writer uses, good writing should remain consistent throughout. If the writer chooses to include the tragic, personal experience above, it would affect the style, tone, and mood of the entire text. It would seem out of place for such an example to be used in the middle of a neutral, measured, and analytical text. To adjust the rest of the text, the writer needs to make additional choices to remain consistent. For example, the writer might decide to use the word *tragedy* in place of the more neutral *fatality*, or they could describe a series of car-related deaths as an *epidemic*. Adverbs and adjectives such as *devastating* or *horribly* could be included to maintain this consistent attitude toward the content. When analyzing writing, look for sudden shifts in style, tone, and mood, and consider whether the writer would be wiser to maintain the prevailing strategy.

Interpret Influences of Historical Context

Studying historical literature is fascinating. It reveals a snapshot in time of people, places, and cultures; a collective set of beliefs and attitudes that no longer exist. Writing changes as attitudes and cultures evolve. Beliefs previously considered immoral or wrong may be considered acceptable today. Researching the historical period of an author gives the reader perspective. The dialogue in Jane Austen's *Pride and Prejudice*, for example, is indicative of social class during the Regency era. Similarly, the stereotypes and slurs in *The Adventures of Huckleberry Finn* were a result of common attitudes and beliefs in the late 1800s, attitudes now found to be reprehensible.

Recognizing Cultural Themes

Regardless of culture, place, or time, certain themes are universal to the human condition. Because humans experience joy, rage, jealousy, and pride, certain themes span centuries. For example, Shakespeare's *Macbeth,* as well as modern works like *The 50th Law* by rapper 50 Cent and Robert Greene or the Netflix series *House of Cards* all feature characters who commit atrocious acts because of ambition. Similarly, *The Adventures of Huckleberry Finn*, published in the 1880s, and *The Catcher in the Rye*, published in the 1950s, both have characters who lie, connive, and survive on their wits.

Moviegoers know whether they are seeing an action, romance or horror film, and are often disappointed if the movie doesn't fit into the conventions of a particular category. Similarly, categories or genres give readers a sense of what to expect from a text. Some of the most basic genres in literature include books, short stories, poetry, and drama. Many genres can be split into sub-genres. For example, the sub-genres of historical fiction, realistic fiction, and fantasy all fit under the fiction genre.

Each genre has a unique way of approaching a particular theme. Books and short stories use plot, characterization, and setting, while poems rely on figurative language, sound devices, and symbolism. Dramas reveal plot through dialogue and the actor's voice and body language.

Main Ideas and Supporting Details

It is very important to know the difference between the topic and the main idea of the text. Even though these two are similar because they both present the central point of a text, they have distinctive differences. A *topic* is the subject of the text; it can usually be described in a one- to two-word phrase and appears in the simplest form. On the other hand, the *main idea* is more detailed and provides the author's central point of the text. It can be expressed through a complete sentence and can be found in the beginning, middle, or end of a paragraph. In most nonfiction books, the first sentence of the passage usually (but not always) states the main idea. Take a look at the passage below to review the topic versus the main idea.

Cheetahs

Cheetahs are one of the fastest mammals on land, reaching up to 70 miles an hour over short distances. Even though cheetahs can run as fast as 70 miles an hour, they usually only have to run half that speed to catch up with their choice of prey. Cheetahs cannot maintain a fast pace over long periods of time because they will overheat their bodies. After a chase, cheetahs need to rest for approximately 30 minutes prior to eating or returning to any other activity.

In the example above, the topic of the passage is "Cheetahs" simply because that is the subject of the text. The main idea of the text is "Cheetahs are one of the fastest mammals on land but can only maintain this fast pace for short distances." While it covers the topic, it is more detailed and refers to the text in its entirety. The text continues to provide additional details called *supporting details,* which will be discussed in the next section.

Supporting Details

Supporting details help readers better develop and understand the main idea. Supporting details answer questions like *who, what, where, when, why,* and *how.* Different types of supporting details include examples, facts and statistics, anecdotes, and sensory details.

Persuasive and informative texts often use supporting details. In persuasive texts, authors attempt to make readers agree with their point of view, and supporting details are often used as "selling points." If authors make a statement, they should support the statement with evidence in order to adequately persuade readers. Informative texts use supporting details such as examples and facts to inform readers. Take another look at the previous "Cheetahs" passage to find examples of supporting details.

Cheetahs

Cheetahs are one of the fastest mammals on land, reaching up to 70 miles an hour over short distances. Even though cheetahs can run as fast as 70 miles an hour, they usually only have to run half that speed to catch up with their choice of prey. Cheetahs cannot maintain a fast pace over long periods of time because they will overheat their bodies. After a chase, cheetahs need to rest for approximately 30 minutes prior to eating or returning to any other activity.

In the example above, supporting details include:

- Cheetahs reach up to 70 miles per hour over short distances.
- They usually only have to run half that speed to catch up with their prey.
- Cheetahs will overheat their bodies if they exert a high speed over longer distances.
- Cheetahs need to rest for 30 minutes after a chase.

Look at the diagram below (applying the cheetah example) to help determine the hierarchy of topic, main idea, and supporting details.

Drawing Conclusions

Determining conclusions requires being an active reader, as a reader must make a prediction and analyze facts to identify a conclusion. There are a few ways to determine a logical conclusion, but careful reading is the most important. It's helpful to read a passage a few times, noting details that seem important to the piece. A reader should also identify key words in a passage to determine the logical conclusion or determination that flows from the information presented.

Textual evidence within the details helps readers draw a conclusion about a passage. *Textual evidence* refers to information—facts and examples that support the main point. Textual evidence will likely come from outside sources and can be in the form of quoted or paraphrased material. In order to draw a conclusion from evidence, it's important to examine the credibility and validity of that evidence as well as how (and if) it relates to the main idea.

If an author presents a differing opinion or a *counter-argument* in order to refute it, the reader should consider how and why this information is being presented. It is meant to strengthen the original argument and shouldn't be confused with the author's intended conclusion, but it should also be considered in the reader's final evaluation.

Sometimes, authors explicitly state the conclusion they want readers to understand. Alternatively, a conclusion may not be directly stated. In that case, readers must rely on the implications to form a logical conclusion:

> On the way to the bus stop, Michael realized his homework wasn't in his backpack. He ran back to the house to get it and made it back to the bus just in time.

In this example, though it's never explicitly stated, it can be inferred that Michael is a student on his way to school in the morning. When forming a conclusion from implied information, it's important to read the text carefully to find several pieces of evidence in the text to support the conclusion.

Summarizing is an effective way to draw a conclusion from a passage. A summary is a shortened version of the original text, written by the reader in his/her own words. Focusing on the main points of the original text and including only the relevant details can help readers reach a conclusion. It's important to retain the original meaning of the passage.

Like summarizing, *paraphrasing* can also help a reader fully understand different parts of a text. Paraphrasing calls for the reader to take a small part of the passage and list or describe its main points. Paraphrasing is more than rewording the original passage, though. It should be written in the reader's own words, while still retaining the meaning of the original source. This will indicate an understanding of the original source, yet still help the reader expand on his/her interpretation.

Readers should pay attention to the *sequence*, or the order in which details are laid out in the text, as this can be important to understanding its meaning as a whole. Writers will often use transitional words to help the reader understand the order of events and to stay on track. Words like *next, then, after*, and *finally* show that the order of events is important to the author. In some cases, the author omits these transitional words, and the sequence is implied. Authors may even purposely present the information out of order to make an impact or have an effect on the reader. An example might be when a narrative writer uses *flashback* to reveal information.

There are several ways readers can draw conclusions from authors' ideas, such as note taking, text evidence, text credibility, writing a response to text, directly stated information versus implications, outlining, summarizing, and paraphrasing. Let's take a look at each important strategy to help readers draw logical conclusions.

Note Taking
When readers take notes throughout texts or passages, they are jotting down important facts or points that the author makes. Note taking is a useful record of information that helps readers understand the text or passage and respond to it. When taking notes, readers should keep lines brief and filled with pertinent information so that they are not rereading a large amount of text, but rather just key points, elements, or words. After readers have completed a text or passage, they can refer to their notes to help them form a conclusion about the author's ideas in the text or passage.

Text Evidence
Text evidence is the information readers find in a text or passage that supports the main idea or point(s) in a story. In turn, text evidence can help readers draw conclusions about the text or passage. The information should be taken directly from the text or passage and placed in quotation marks. Text evidence provides readers with information to support ideas about the text so that they do not rely

simply on their own thoughts. Details should be precise, descriptive, and factual. Statistics are a great piece of text evidence because they provide readers with exact numbers and not just a generalization. For example, instead of saying "Asia has a larger population than Europe," authors could provide detailed information such as, "In Asia there are over 4 billion people, whereas in Europe there are a little over 750 million." More definitive information provides better evidence to readers to help support their conclusions about texts or passages.

Text Credibility

Credible sources are important when drawing conclusions because readers need to be able to trust what they are reading. Authors should always use credible sources to help gain the trust of their readers. A text is *credible* when it is believable and the author is objective and unbiased. If readers do not trust an author's words, they may simply dismiss the text completely. For example, if an author writes a persuasive essay, he or she is outwardly trying to sway readers' opinions to align with his or her own. Readers may agree or disagree with the author, which may, in turn, lead them to believe that the author is credible or not credible. Also, readers should keep in mind the source of the text. If readers review a journal about astronomy, would a more reliable source be a NASA employee or a medical doctor? Overall, text credibility is important when drawing conclusions, because readers want reliable sources that support the decisions they have made about the author's ideas.

Writing a Response to Text

Once readers have determined their opinions and validated the credibility of a text, they can then reflect on the text. Writing a response to a text is one way readers can reflect on the given text or passage. When readers write responses to a text, it is important for them to rely on the evidence within the text to support their opinions or thoughts. Supporting evidence such as facts, details, statistics, and quotes directly from the text are key pieces of information readers should reflect upon or use when writing a response to text.

Directly Stated Information Versus Implications

Engaged readers should constantly self-question while reviewing texts to help them form conclusions. Self-questioning is when readers review a paragraph, page, passage, or chapter and ask themselves, "Did I understand what I read?," "What was the main event in this section?," "Where is this taking place?," and so on. Authors can provide clues or pieces of evidence throughout a text or passage to guide readers toward a conclusion. This is why active and engaged readers should read the text or passage in its entirety before forming a definitive conclusion. If readers do not gather all the pieces of evidence needed, then they may jump to an illogical conclusion.

At times, authors directly state conclusions while others simply imply them. Of course, it is easier if authors outwardly provide conclusions to readers, because it does not leave any information open to interpretation. On the other hand, implications are things that authors do not directly state but can be assumed based off of information they provided. If authors only imply what may have happened, readers can form a menagerie of ideas for conclusions. For example, look at the following statement: "Once we heard the sirens, we hunkered down in the storm shelter." In this statement, the author does not directly state that there was a tornado, but clues such as "sirens" and "storm shelter" provide insight to the readers to help form that conclusion.

Outlining

An outline is a system used to organize writing. When reading texts, outlining is important because it helps readers organize important information in a logical pattern using roman numerals. Usually, outlines start with the main idea(s) and then branch out into subgroups or subsidiary thoughts of subjects. Not only do outlines provide a visual tool for readers to reflect on how events, characters, settings, or other key parts of the text or passage relate to one another, but they can also lead readers to a stronger conclusion.

The sample below demonstrates what a general outline looks like.

Sample Outline
  I.   Main Topic 1
         a. Subtopic 1
         b. Subtopic 2
              1. Detail 1
              2. Detail 2
  II.   Main Topic 2
         a. Subtopic 1
         b. Subtopic 2
              1. Detail 1
              2. Detail 2

Summarizing

At the end of a text or passage, it is important to summarize what the readers read. Summarizing is a strategy in which readers determine what is important throughout the text or passage, shorten those ideas, and rewrite or retell it in their own words. A summary should identify the main idea of the text or passage. Important details or supportive evidence should also be accurately reported in the summary. If writers provide irrelevant details in the summary, it may cloud the greater meaning of the summary in the text. When summarizing, writers should not include their opinions, quotes, or what they thought the author should have said. A clear summary provides clarity of the text or passage to the readers. Let's review the checklist of items writers should include in their summary.

Summary Checklist
- Title of the story
- Someone: Who is or are the main character(s)?
- Wanted: What did the character(s) want?
- But: What was the problem?
- So: How did the character(s) solve the problem?
- Then: How did the story end? What was the resolution?

Paraphrasing

Another strategy readers can use to help them fully comprehend a text or passage is paraphrasing. Paraphrasing is when readers take the author's words and put them into their own words. When readers and writers paraphrase, they should avoid copying the text—that is plagiarism. It is also important to include as many details as possible when restating the facts. Not only will this help readers and writers recall information, but by putting the information into their own words, they demonstrate whether or not they fully comprehend the text or passage. Look at the example below showing an original text and how to paraphrase it.

Original Text: Fenway Park is home to the beloved Boston Red Sox. The stadium opened on April 20, 1912. The stadium currently seats over 37,000 fans, many of whom travel from all over the country to experience the iconic team and nostalgia of Fenway Park.

Paraphrased: On April 20, 1912, Fenway Park opened. Home to the Boston Red Sox, the stadium now seats over 37,000 fans. Many spectators travel to watch the Red Sox and experience the spirit of Fenway Park.

Paraphrasing, summarizing, and quoting can often cross paths with one another. Review the chart below showing the similarities and differences between the three strategies.

Paraphrasing	Summarizing	Quoting
Uses own words	Puts main ideas into own words	Uses words that are identical to text
References original source	References original source	Requires quotation marks
Uses own sentences	Shows important ideas of source	Uses author's own words and ideas

Inferences in a Text

Readers should be able to make *inferences*. Making an inference requires the reader to read between the lines and look for what is *implied* rather than what is directly stated. That is, using information that is known from the text, the reader is able to make a logical assumption about information that is *not* directly stated but is probably true. Read the following passage:

"Hey, do you wanna meet my new puppy?" Jonathan asked.

"Oh, I'm sorry but please don't—" Jacinta began to protest, but before she could finish, Jonathan had already opened the passenger side door of his car and a perfect white ball of fur came bouncing towards Jacinta.

"Isn't he the cutest?" beamed Jonathan.

"Yes—achoo!—he's pretty—aaaachooo!!—adora—aaa—aaaachoo!" Jacinta managed to say in between sneezes. "But if you don't mind, I—I—achoo!—need to go inside."

Which of the following can be inferred from Jacinta's reaction to the puppy?
　　a. she hates animals
　　b. she is allergic to dogs
　　c. she prefers cats to dogs
　　d. she is angry at Jonathan

An inference requires the reader to consider the information presented and then form their own idea about what is probably true. Based on the details in the passage, what is the best answer to the question? Important details to pay attention to include the tone of Jacinta's dialogue, which is overall polite and apologetic, as well as her reaction itself, which is a long string of sneezes. Answer choices (a) and (d) both express strong emotions ("hates" and "angry") that are not evident in Jacinta's speech or actions. Answer choice (c) mentions cats, but there is nothing in the passage to indicate Jacinta's feelings about cats. Answer choice (b), "she is allergic to dogs," is the most logical choice—based on the fact that she began sneezing as soon as a fluffy dog approached her, it makes sense to guess that Jacinta might be allergic to dogs. So even though Jacinta never directly states, "Sorry, I'm allergic to dogs!" using the clues in the passage, it is still reasonable to guess that this is true.

Making inferences is crucial for readers of literature, because literary texts often avoid presenting complete and direct information to readers about characters' thoughts or feelings, or they present this information in an unclear way, leaving it up to the reader to interpret clues given in the text. In order to make inferences while reading, readers should ask themselves:

- What details are being presented in the text?
- Is there any important information that seems to be missing?
- Based on the information that the author *does* include, what else is probably true?
- Is this inference reasonable based on what is already known?

Apply Information

A natural extension of being able to make an inference from a given set of information is also being able to apply that information to a new context. This is especially useful in non-fiction or informative writing. Considering the facts and details presented in the text, readers should consider how the same information might be relevant in a different situation. The following is an example of applying an inferential conclusion to a different context:

> Often, individuals behave differently in large groups than they do as individuals. One example of this is the psychological phenomenon known as the bystander effect. According to the bystander effect, the more people who witness an accident or crime occur, the less likely each individual bystander is to respond or offer assistance to the victim. A classic example of this is the murder of Kitty Genovese in New York City in the 1960s. Although there were over thirty witnesses to her killing by a stabber, none of them intervened to help Kitty or contact the police.

Considering the phenomenon of the bystander effect, what would probably happen if somebody tripped on the stairs in a crowded subway station?
a. Everybody would stop to help the person who tripped
b. Bystanders would point and laugh at the person who tripped
c. Someone would call the police after walking away from the station
d. Few if any bystanders would offer assistance to the person who tripped

This question asks readers to apply the information they learned from the passage, which is an informative paragraph about the bystander effect. According to the passage, this is a concept in psychology that describes the way people in groups respond to an accident—the more people are present, the less likely any one person is to intervene. While the passage illustrates this effect with the example of a woman's murder, the question asks readers to apply it to a different context—in this case, someone falling down the stairs in front of many subway passengers. Although this specific situation is not discussed in the passage, readers should be able to apply the general concepts described in the paragraph. The definition of the bystander effect includes any instance of an accident or crime in front of a large group of people. The question asks about a situation that falls within the same definition, so the general concept should still hold true: in the midst of a large crowd, few individuals are likely to actually respond to an accident. In this case, answer choice (d) is the best response.

Critical Thinking Skills

It's important to read any piece of writing critically. The goal is to discover the point and purpose of what the author is writing about through analysis. It's also crucial to establish the point or stance the author has taken on the topic of the piece. After determining the author's perspective, readers can then more effectively develop their own viewpoints on the subject of the piece.

It is important to distinguish between *fact and opinion* when reading a piece of writing. A fact is information that can be proven true. If information can be disproved, it is not a fact. For example, water freezes at or below thirty-two degrees Fahrenheit. An argument stating that water freezes at seventy degrees Fahrenheit cannot be supported by data, and is therefore not a fact. Facts tend to be associated with science, mathematics, and statistics. Opinions are information open to debate. Opinions are often tied to subjective concepts like equality, morals, and rights. They can also be controversial. An affirmative argument for a position—such as gun control—can be just as effective as an opposing argument against it.

Authors often use words like *think, feel, believe,* or *in my opinion* when expressing opinion, but these words won't always appear in an opinion piece, especially if it is formally written. An author's opinion may be backed up by facts, which gives it more credibility, but that opinion should not be taken as fact. A critical reader should be suspect of an author's opinion, especially if it is only supported by other opinions.

Fact	Opinion
There are 9 innings in a game of baseball.	Baseball games run too long.
James Garfield was assassinated on July 2, 1881.	James Garfield was a good president.
McDonalds has stores in 118 countries.	McDonalds has the best hamburgers.

Critical readers examine the facts used to support an author's argument. They check the facts against other sources to be sure those facts are correct. They also check the validity of the sources used to be sure those sources are credible, academic, and/or peer- reviewed. Consider that when an author uses another person's opinion to support his or her argument, even if it is an expert's opinion, it is still only an opinion and should not be taken as fact. A strong argument uses valid, measurable facts to support ideas. Even then, the reader may disagree with the argument as it may be rooted in his or her personal beliefs.

An authoritative argument may use the facts to sway the reader. In the example of global warming, many experts differ in their opinions of what alternative fuels can be used to aid in offsetting it. Because of this, a writer may choose to only use the information and expert opinion that supports his or her viewpoint.

If the argument is that wind energy is the best solution, the author will use facts that support this idea. That same author may leave out relevant facts on solar energy. The way the author uses facts can influence the reader, so it's important to consider the facts being used, how those facts are being presented, and what information might be left out.

Critical readers should also look for errors in the argument such as logical fallacies and bias. A *logical fallacy* is a flaw in the logic used to make the argument. Logical fallacies include slippery slope, straw man, and begging the question. Authors can also reflect *bias* if they ignore an opposing viewpoint or present their side in an unbalanced way. A strong argument considers the opposition and finds a way to refute it. Critical readers should look for an unfair or one-sided presentation of the argument and be skeptical, as a bias may be present. Even if this bias is unintentional, if it exists in the writing, the reader should be wary of the validity of the argument.

Readers should also look for the use of *stereotypes,* which refer to specific groups. Stereotypes are often negative connotations about a person or place and should always be avoided. When a critical reader finds stereotypes in a piece of writing, they should immediately be critical of the argument and consider the validity of anything the author presents. Stereotypes reveal a flaw in the writer's thinking and may suggest a lack of knowledge or understanding about the subject.

Author's Use of Language

Authors utilize a wide range of techniques to tell a story or communicate information. Readers should be familiar with the most common of these techniques. Techniques of writing are also commonly known as rhetorical devices.

Types of Appeals

In non-fiction writing, authors employ argumentative techniques to present their opinion to readers in the most convincing way. First of all, persuasive writing usually includes at least one type of appeal: an appeal to logic (logos), emotion (pathos), or credibility and trustworthiness (ethos). When a writer appeals to logic, they are asking readers to agree with them based on research, evidence, and an established line of reasoning. An author's argument might also appeal to readers' emotions, perhaps by including personal stories and anecdotes (a short narrative of a specific event). A final type of appeal, appeal to authority, asks the reader to agree with the author's argument on the basis of their expertise or credentials. Consider three different approaches to arguing the same opinion:

Logic (Logos)
This is an example of an appeal to logic:

> Our school should abolish its current ban on cell phone use on campus. This rule was adopted last year as an attempt to reduce class disruptions and help students focus more on their lessons. However, since the rule was enacted, there has been no change in the number of disciplinary problems in class. Therefore, the rule is ineffective and should be done away with.

The author uses evidence to disprove the logic of the school's rule (the rule was supposed to reduce discipline problems; the number of problems has not been reduced; therefore, the rule is not working) and call for its repeal.

Emotion (Pathos)
An author's argument might also appeal to readers' emotions, perhaps by including personal stories and anecdotes. The next example presents an appeal to emotion. By sharing the personal anecdote of one student and speaking about emotional topics like family relationships, the author invokes the reader's empathy in asking them to reconsider the school rule.

Our school should abolish its current ban on cell phone use on campus. If they aren't able to use their phones during the school day, many students feel isolated from their loved ones. For example, last semester, one student's grandmother had a heart attack in the morning. However, because he couldn't use his cell phone, the student didn't know about his grandmother's accident until the end of the day—when she had already passed away and it was too late to say goodbye. By preventing students from contacting their friends and family, our school is placing undue stress and anxiety on students.

Credibility (Ethos)

Finally, an appeal to authority includes a statement from a relevant expert. In this case, the author uses a doctor in the field of education to support the argument. All three examples begin from the same opinion—the school's phone ban needs to change—but rely on different argumentative styles to persuade the reader.

Our school should abolish its current ban on cell phone use on campus. According to Dr. Bartholomew Everett, a leading educational expert, "Research studies show that cell phone usage has no real impact on student attentiveness. Rather, phones provide a valuable technological resource for learning. Schools need to learn how to integrate this new technology into their curriculum." Rather than banning phones altogether, our school should follow the advice of experts and allow students to use phones as part of their learning.

Rhetorical Questions

Another commonly used argumentative technique is asking rhetorical questions, questions that do not actually require an answer but that push the reader to consider the topic further.

I wholly disagree with the proposal to ban restaurants from serving foods with high sugar and sodium contents. Do we really want to live in a world where the government can control what we eat? I prefer to make my own food choices.

Here, the author's rhetorical question prompts readers to put themselves in a hypothetical situation and imagine how they would feel about it.

Figurative Language

Literary texts also employ rhetorical devices. Figurative language like simile and metaphor is a type of rhetorical device commonly found in literature. In addition to rhetorical devices that play on the *meanings* of words, there are also rhetorical devices that use the *sounds* of words. These devices are most often found in poetry, but may also be found in other types of literature and in non-fiction writing like speech texts.

Alliteration and *assonance* are both varieties of sound repetition. Other types of sound repetition include: anaphora, repetition that occurs at the beginning of the sentences; epiphora, repetition occurring at the end of phrases; antimetabole, repetition of words in reverse order; and antiphrasis, a form of denial of an assertion in a text.

Alliteration refers to the repetition of the first sound of each word. Recall Robert Burns' opening line:

My love is like a red, red rose

This line includes two instances of alliteration: "love" and "like" (repeated *L* sound), as well as "red" and "rose" (repeated *R* sound). Next, assonance refers to the repetition of vowel sounds, and can occur anywhere within a word (not just the opening sound). Here is the opening of a poem by John Keats:

> When I have fears that I may cease to be
>
> Before my pen has glean'd my teeming brain

Assonance can be found in the words "fears," "cease," "be," "glean'd," and "teeming," all of which stress the long *E* sound. Both alliteration and assonance create a harmony that unifies the writer's language.

Another sound device is *onomatopoeia*, or words whose spelling mimics the sound they describe. Words like "crash," "bang," and "sizzle" are all examples of onomatopoeia. Use of onomatopoetic language adds auditory imagery to the text.

Readers are probably most familiar with the technique of *pun*. A pun is a play on words, taking advantage of two words that have the same or similar pronunciation. Puns can be found throughout Shakespeare's plays, for instance:

> Now is the winter of our discontent
> Made glorious summer by this son of York

These lines from *Richard III* contain a play on words. Richard III refers to his brother, the newly crowned King Edward IV, as the "son of York," referencing their family heritage from the house of York. However, while drawing a comparison between the political climate and the weather (times of political trouble were the "winter," but now the new king brings "glorious summer"), Richard's use of the word "son" also implies another word with the same pronunciation, "sun"—so Edward IV is also like the sun, bringing light, warmth, and hope to England. Puns are a clever way for writers to suggest two meanings at once.

Counterarguments

If an author presents a differing opinion or a counterargument in order to refute it, the reader should consider how and why this information is being presented. It is meant to strengthen the original argument and shouldn't be confused with the author's intended conclusion, but it should also be considered in the reader's final evaluation.

Authors can also use bias if they ignore the opposing viewpoint or present their side in an unbalanced way. A strong argument considers the opposition and finds a way to refute it. Critical readers should look for an unfair or one-sided presentation of the argument and be skeptical, as a bias may be present. Even if this bias is unintentional, if it exists in the writing, the reader should be wary of the validity of the argument. Readers should also look for the use of stereotypes, which refer to specific groups. Stereotypes are often negative connotations about a person or place, and should always be avoided. When a critical reader finds stereotypes in a piece of writing, they should be critical of the argument, and consider the validity of anything the author presents. Stereotypes reveal a flaw in the writer's thinking and may suggest a lack of knowledge or understanding about the subject.

Meaning of Words in Context

There will be many occasions in one's reading career in which an unknown word or a word with multiple meanings will pop up. There are ways of determining what these words or phrases mean that do not require the use of the dictionary, which is especially helpful during a test where one may not be available. Even outside of the exam, knowing how to derive an understanding of a word via context clues will be a critical skill in the real world. The context is the circumstances in which a story or a passage is happening, and can usually be found in the series of words directly before or directly after the word or phrase in question. The clues are the words that hint towards the meaning of the unknown word or phrase.

There may be questions that ask about the meaning of a particular word or phrase within a passage. There are a couple ways to approach these kinds of questions:

1. Define the word or phrase in a way that is easy to comprehend (using context clues).
2. Try out each answer choice in place of the word.

To demonstrate, here's an example from *Alice in Wonderland*:

Alice was beginning to get very tired of sitting by her sister on the bank, and of having nothing to do: once or twice she peeped into the book her sister was reading, but it had no pictures or conversations in it, "and what is the use of a book," thought Alice, "without pictures or conversations?"

Q: As it is used in the selection, the word peeped means:

Using the first technique, before looking at the answers, define the word "peeped" using context clues and then find the matching answer. Then, analyze the entire passage in order to determine the meaning, not just the surrounding words.

To begin, imagine a blank where the word should be and put a synonym or definition there: "once or twice she _____ into the book her sister was reading." The context clue here is the book. It may be tempting to put "read" where the blank is, but notice the preposition word, "into." One does not read *into* a book, one simply reads a book, and since reading a book requires that it is seen with a pair of eyes, then "look" would make the most sense to put into the blank: "once or twice she looked into the book her sister was reading."

Once an easy-to-understand word or synonym has been supplanted, readers should check to make sure it makes sense with the rest of the passage. What happened after she looked into the book? She thought to herself how a book without pictures or conversations is useless. This situation in its entirety makes sense.

Now check the answer choices for a match:
   a. To make a high-pitched cry
   b. To smack
   c. To look curiously
   d. To pout

Since the word was already defined, Choice *C* is the best option.

Using the second technique, replace the figurative blank with each of the answer choices and determine which one is the most appropriate. Remember to look further into the passage to clarify that they work, because they could still make sense out of context.

    a. Once or twice she <u>made a high pitched cry</u> into the book her sister was reading
    b. Once or twice she <u>smacked</u> into the book her sister was reading
    c. Once or twice she <u>looked curiously</u> into the book her sister was reading
    d. Once or twice she <u>pouted</u> into the book her sister was reading

For Choice *A*, it does not make much sense in any context for a person to yell into a book, unless maybe something terrible has happened in the story. Given that afterward Alice thinks to herself how useless a book without pictures is, this option does not make sense within context.

For Choice *B*, smacking a book someone is reading may make sense if the rest of the passage indicates a reason for doing so. If Alice was angry or her sister had shoved it in her face, then maybe smacking the book would make sense within context. However, since whatever she does with the book causes her to think, "what is the use of a book without pictures or conversations?" then answer Choice *B* is not an appropriate answer. Answer Choice *C* fits well within context, given her subsequent thoughts on the matter. Answer Choice *D* does not make sense in context or grammatically, as people do not "pout into" things.

This is a simple example to illustrate the techniques outlined above. There may, however, be a question in which all of the definitions are correct and also make sense out of context, in which the appropriate context clues will really need to be honed in on in order to determine the correct answer. For example, here is another passage from *Alice in Wonderland*:

> . . . but when the Rabbit actually took a watch out of its waistcoat pocket, and looked at it, and then hurried on, Alice <u>started</u> to her feet, for it flashed across her mind that she had never before seen a rabbit with either a waistcoat-pocket or a watch to take out of it, and burning with curiosity, she ran across the field after it, and was just in time to see it pop down a large rabbit-hole under the hedge.

Q: As it is used in the passage, the word started means
    a. To turn on
    b. To begin
    c. To move quickly
    d. To be surprised

All of these words qualify as a definition of "start," but using context clues, the correct answer can be identified using one of the two techniques above. It's easy to see that one does not turn on, begin, or be surprised to one's feet. The selection also states that she "ran across the field after it," indicating that she was in a hurry. Therefore, to move quickly would make the most sense in this context.

The same strategies can be applied to vocabulary that may be completely unfamiliar. In this case, focus on the words before or after the unknown word in order to determine its definition. Take this sentence, for example:

> Sam was such a <u>miser</u> that he forced Andrew to pay him twelve cents for the candy, even though he had a large inheritance and he knew his friend was poor.

Unlike with assertion questions, for vocabulary questions, it may be necessary to apply some critical thinking skills that may not be explicitly stated within the passage. Think about the implications of the passage, or what the text is trying to say. With this example, it is important to realize that it is considered unusually stingy for a person to demand so little money from someone instead of just letting their friend have the candy, especially if this person is already wealthy. Hence, a <u>miser</u> is a greedy or stingy individual.

Questions about complex vocabulary may not be explicitly asked, but this is a useful skill to know. If there is an unfamiliar word while reading a passage and its definition goes unknown, it is possible to miss out on a critical message that could inhibit the ability to appropriately answer the questions. Practicing this technique in daily life will sharpen this ability to derive meanings from context clues with ease.

Practice Test

Directions for questions 1–9: Read the statement or passage and then choose the best answer to the question. Answer the question based on what is stated or implied in the statement or passage.

1. There are two major kinds of cameras on the market right now for amateur photographers. Camera enthusiasts can either purchase a digital single-lens reflex camera (DSLR) camera or a compact system camera (CSC). The main difference between a DSLR and a CSC is that the DSLR has a full-sized sensor, which means it fits in a much larger body. The CSC uses a mirrorless system, which makes for a lighter, smaller camera. While both take quality pictures, the DSLR generally has better picture quality due to the larger sensor. CSCs still take very good quality pictures and are more convenient to carry than a DSLR. This makes the CSC an ideal choice for the amateur photographer looking to step up from a point-and-shoot camera.

What is the main difference between the DSLR and CSC?
    a. The picture quality is better in the DSLR.
    b. The CSC is less expensive than the DSLR.
    c. The DSLR is a better choice for amateur photographers.
    d. The DSLR's larger sensor makes it a bigger camera than the CSC.

2. When selecting a career path, it's important to explore the various options available. Many students entering college may shy away from a major because they don't know much about it. For example, many students won't opt for a career as an actuary, because they aren't exactly sure what it entails. They would be missing out on a career that is very lucrative and in high demand. Actuaries work in the insurance field and assess risks and premiums. The average salary of an actuary is $100,000 per year. Another career option students may avoid, due to lack of knowledge of the field, is a hospitalist. This is a physician that specializes in the care of patients in a hospital, as opposed to those seen in private practices. The average salary of a hospitalist is upwards of $200,000. It pays to do some digging and find out more about these lesser-known career fields.

What is an actuary?
    a. A doctor who works in a hospital.
    b. The same as a hospitalist.
    c. An insurance agent who works in a hospital.
    d. A person who assesses insurance risks and premiums.

3. Hard water occurs when rainwater mixes with minerals from rock and soil. Hard water has a high mineral count, including calcium and magnesium. The mineral deposits from hard water can stain hard surfaces in bathrooms and kitchens as well as clog pipes. Hard water can stain dishes, ruin clothes, and reduce the life of any appliances it touches, such as hot water heaters, washing machines, and humidifiers.

One solution is to install a water softener to reduce the mineral content of water, but this can be costly. Running vinegar through pipes and appliances and using vinegar to clean hard surfaces can also help with mineral deposits.

From this passage, what can be concluded?
    a. Hard water can cause a lot of problems for homeowners.
    b. Calcium is good for pipes and hard surfaces.
    c. Water softeners are easy to install.
    d. Vinegar is the only solution to hard water problems.

4. Coaches of kids' sports teams are increasingly concerned about the behavior of parents at games. Parents are screaming and cursing at coaches, officials, players, and other parents. Physical fights have even broken out at games. Parents need to be reminded that coaches are volunteers, giving up their time and energy to help kids develop in their chosen sport. The goal of kids' sports teams is to learn and develop skills, but it's also to have fun. When parents are out of control at games and practices, it takes the fun out of the sport.

From this passage, what can be concluded?
    a. Coaches are modeling good behavior for kids.
    b. Organized sports are not good for kids.
    c. Parents' behavior at their kids' games needs to change.
    d. Parents and coaches need to work together.

5. While scientists aren't entirely certain why tornadoes form, they have some clues into the process. Tornadoes are dangerous funnel clouds that occur during a large thunderstorm. When warm, humid air near the ground meets cold, dry air from above, a column of the warm air can be drawn up into the clouds. Winds at different altitudes blowing at different speeds make the column of air rotate. As the spinning column of air picks up speed, a funnel cloud is formed. This funnel cloud moves rapidly and haphazardly. Rain and hail inside the cloud cause it to touch down, creating a tornado. Tornadoes move in a rapid and unpredictable pattern, making them extremely destructive and dangerous. Scientists continue to study tornadoes to improve radar detection and warning times.

The main purpose of this passage is to do which of the following?
    a. Show why tornadoes are dangerous.
    b. Explain how a tornado forms.
    c. Compare thunderstorms to tornadoes.
    d. Explain what to do in the event of a tornado.

6. Many people are unsure of exactly how the digestive system works. Digestion begins in the mouth where teeth grind up food and saliva breaks it down, making it easier for the body to absorb. Next, the food moves to the esophagus, and it is pushed into the stomach. The stomach is where food is stored and broken down further by acids and digestive enzymes, preparing it for passage into the intestines. The small intestine is where the nutrients are taken from food and passed into the blood stream. Other essential organs like the liver, gall bladder, and pancreas aid the stomach in breaking down food and absorbing nutrients. Finally, food waste is passed into the large intestine where it is eliminated by the body.

The purpose of this passage is to do which of the following?
    a. Explain how the liver works.
    b. Show why it is important to eat healthy foods.
    c. Explain how the digestive system works.
    d. Show how nutrients are absorbed by the small intestine.

7. Osteoporosis is a medical condition that occurs when the body loses bone or makes too little bone. This can lead to brittle, fragile bones that easily break. Bones are already porous, and when osteoporosis sets in, the spaces in bones become much larger, causing them to weaken. Both men and women can contract osteoporosis, though it is most common in women over age 50. Loss of bone can be silent and progressive, so it is important to be proactive in prevention of the disease.

The main purpose of this passage is to do which of the following?
    a. Discuss some of the ways people contract osteoporosis.
    b. Describe different treatment options for those with osteoporosis.
    c. Explain how to prevent osteoporosis.
    d. Define osteoporosis.

8. Vacationers looking for a perfect experience should opt out of Disney parks and try a trip on Disney Cruise Lines. While a park offers rides, characters, and show experiences, it also includes long lines, often very hot weather, and enormous crowds. A Disney Cruise, on the other hand, is a relaxing, luxurious vacation that includes many of the same experiences as the parks, minus the crowds and lines. The cruise has top-notch food, maid service, water slides, multiple pools, Broadway-quality shows, and daily character experiences for kids. There are also many activities, such as bingo, trivia contests, and dance parties that can entertain guests of all ages. The cruise even stops at Disney's private island for a beach barbecue with characters, waterslides, and water sports. Those looking for the Disney experience without the hassle should book a Disney cruise.

The main purpose of this passage is to do which of the following?
    a. Explain how to book a Disney cruise.
    b. Show what Disney parks have to offer.
    c. Show why Disney parks are expensive.
    d. Compare Disney parks to the Disney cruise.

9. As summer approaches, drowning incidents will increase. Drowning happens very quickly and silently. Most people assume that drowning is easy to spot, but a person who is drowning doesn't make noise or wave their arms. Instead, they will have their head back and their mouth open, with just the face out of the water. A person who is truly in danger of drowning is not able to wave their arms in the air or move much at all. Recognizing these signs of drowning can prevent tragedy.

The main purpose of this passage is to do which of the following?
  a. Explain the dangers of swimming.
  b. Show how to identify the signs of drowning.
  c. Explain how to be a lifeguard.
  d. Compare the signs of drowning.

The next question is based on the following conversation between a scientist and a politician.

> Scientist: Last year was the warmest ever recorded in the last 134 years. During that time period, the ten warmest years have all occurred since 2000. This correlates directly with the recent increases in carbon dioxide as large countries like China, India, and Brazil continue developing and industrializing. No longer do just a handful of countries burn massive amounts of carbon-based fossil fuels; it is quickly becoming the case throughout the whole world as technology and industry spread.

> Politician: Yes, but there is no causal link between increases in carbon emissions and increasing temperatures. The link is tenuous and nothing close to certain. We need to wait for all of the data before drawing hasty conclusions. For all we know, the temperature increase could be entirely natural. I believe the temperatures also rose dramatically during the dinosaurs' time, and I do not think they were burning any fossil fuels back then.

10. What is one point on which the scientist and politician agree?
  a. Burning fossil fuels causes global temperatures to rise.
  b. Global temperatures are increasing.
  c. Countries must revisit their energy policies before it's too late.
  d. Earth's climate naturally goes through warming and cooling periods.

The next question is based on the following passage.

> A famous children's author recently published a historical fiction novel under a pseudonym; however, it did not sell as many copies as her children's books. In her earlier years, she had majored in history and earned a graduate degree in Antebellum American History, which is the time frame of her new novel. Critics praised this newest work far more than the children's series that made her famous. In fact, her new novel was nominated for the prestigious Albert J. Beveridge Award, but still isn't selling like her children's books, which fly off the shelves because of her name alone.

11. Which one of the following statements might be accurately inferred based on the above passage?
  a. The famous children's author produced an inferior book under her pseudonym.
  b. The famous children's author is the foremost expert on Antebellum America.
  c. The famous children's author did not receive the bump in publicity for her historical novel that it would have received if it were written under her given name.
  d. People generally prefer to read children's series than historical fiction.

The next three questions are based on the following passage.

Smoking is Terrible

Smoking tobacco products is terribly destructive. A single cigarette contains over 4,000 chemicals, including 43 known carcinogens and 400 deadly toxins. Some of the most dangerous ingredients include tar, carbon monoxide, formaldehyde, ammonia, arsenic, and DDT. Smoking can cause numerous types of cancer including throat, mouth, nasal cavity, esophagus, stomach, pancreas, kidney, bladder, and cervical.

Cigarettes contain a drug called nicotine, one of the most addictive substances known to man. Addiction is defined as a compulsion to seek the substance despite negative consequences. According to the National Institute of Drug Abuse, nearly 35 million smokers expressed a desire to quit smoking in 2015; however, more than 85 percent of those addicts will not achieve their goal. Almost all smokers regret picking up that first cigarette. You would be wise to learn from their mistake if you have not yet started smoking.

According to the U.S. Department of Health and Human Services, 16 million people in the United States presently suffer from a smoking-related condition and nearly nine million suffer from a serious smoking-related illness. According to the Centers for Disease Control and Prevention (CDC), tobacco products cause nearly six million deaths per year. This number is projected to rise to over eight million deaths by 2030. Smokers, on average, die ten years earlier than their nonsmoking peers.

In the United States, local, state, and federal governments typically tax tobacco products, which leads to high prices. Nicotine addicts sometimes pay more for a pack of cigarettes than for a few gallons of gas. Additionally, smokers tend to stink. The smell of smoke is all-consuming and creates a pervasive nastiness. Smokers also risk staining their teeth and fingers with yellow residue from the tar.

Smoking is deadly, expensive, and socially unappealing. Clearly, smoking is not worth the risks.

12. Which of the following statements most accurately summarizes the passage?
    a. Tobacco is less healthy than many alternatives.
    b. Tobacco is deadly, expensive, and socially unappealing, and smokers would be much better off kicking the addiction.
    c. In the United States, local, state, and federal governments typically tax tobacco products, which leads to high prices.
    d. Tobacco products shorten smokers' lives by ten years and kill more than six million people per year.

13. The author would be most likely to agree with which of the following statements?
    a. Smokers should only quit cold turkey and avoid all nicotine cessation devices.
    b. Other substances are more addictive than tobacco.
    c. Smokers should quit for whatever reason that gets them to stop smoking.
    d. People who want to continue smoking should advocate for a reduction in tobacco product taxes.

14. Which of the following represents an opinion statement on the part of the author?
    a. According to the Centers for Disease Control and Prevention (CDC), tobacco products cause nearly six million deaths per year.
    b. Nicotine addicts sometimes pay more for a pack of cigarettes than a few gallons of gas.
    c. They also risk staining their teeth and fingers with yellow residue from the tar.
    d. Additionally, smokers tend to stink. The smell of smoke is all-consuming and creates a pervasive nastiness.

The next three questions are based on the following passage.

Christopher Columbus is often credited for discovering America. This is incorrect. First, it is impossible to "discover" something where people already live; however, Christopher Columbus did explore places in the New World that were previously untouched by Europe, so the term "explorer" would be more accurate. Another correction must be made, as well: Christopher Columbus was not the first European explorer to reach the present day Americas! Rather, it was Leif Erikson who first came to the New World and contacted the natives, nearly five hundred years before Christopher Columbus.

Leif Erikson, the son of Erik the Red (a famous Viking outlaw and explorer in his own right), was born in either 970 or 980, depending on which historian you seek. His own family, though, did not raise Leif, which was a Viking tradition. Instead, one of Erik's prisoners taught Leif reading and writing, languages, sailing, and weaponry. At age 12, Leif was considered a man and returned to his family. He killed a man during a dispute shortly after his return, and the council banished the Erikson clan to Greenland.

In 999, Leif left Greenland and traveled to Norway where he would serve as a guard to King Olaf Tryggvason. It was there that he became a convert to Christianity. Leif later tried to return home with the intention of taking supplies and spreading Christianity to Greenland, however his ship was blown off course and he arrived in a strange new land: present day Newfoundland, Canada.

When he finally returned to his adopted homeland Greenland, Leif consulted with a merchant who had also seen the shores of this previously unknown land we now know as Canada. The son of the legendary Viking explorer then gathered a crew of 35 men and set sail. Leif became the first European to touch foot in the New World as he explored present-day Baffin Island and Labrador, Canada. His crew called the land Vinland since it was plentiful with grapes.

During their time in present-day Newfoundland, Leif's expedition made contact with the natives whom they referred to as Skraelings (which translates to "wretched ones" in Norse). There are several secondhand accounts of their meetings. Some contemporaries described trade between the peoples. Other accounts describe clashes where the Skraelings defeated the Viking explorers with long spears, while still others claim the Vikings dominated the natives. Regardless of the circumstances, it seems that the Vikings made contact of some kind. This happened around 1000, nearly five hundred years before Columbus famously sailed the ocean blue.

Eventually, in 1003, Leif set sail for home and arrived at Greenland with a ship full of timber. In 1020, seventeen years later, the legendary Viking died. Many believe that Leif Erikson should receive more credit for his contributions in exploring the New World.

15. Which of the following is an opinion, rather than historical fact, expressed by the author?
    a. Leif Erikson was definitely the son of Erik the Red; however, historians debate the year of his birth.
    b. Leif Erikson's crew called the land Vinland since it was plentiful with grapes.
    c. Leif Erikson deserves more credit for his contributions in exploring the New World.
    d. Leif Erikson explored the Americas nearly five hundred years before Christopher Columbus.

16. Which of the following most accurately describes the author's main conclusion?
    a. Leif Erikson is a legendary Viking explorer.
    b. Leif Erikson deserves more credit for exploring America hundreds of years before Columbus.
    c. Spreading Christianity motivated Leif Erikson's expeditions more than any other factor.
    d. Leif Erikson contacted the natives nearly five hundred years before Columbus.

17. Which of the following can be logically inferred from the passage?
    a. The Vikings disliked exploring the New World.
    b. Leif Erikson's banishment from Iceland led to his exploration of present-day Canada.
    c. Leif Erikson never shared his stories of exploration with the King of Norway.
    d. Historians have difficulty definitively pinpointing events in the Vikings' history

This article discusses the famous poet and playwright William Shakespeare. Read it and answer questions 18-21.

People who argue that William Shakespeare is not responsible for the plays attributed to his name are known as anti-Stratfordians (from the name of Shakespeare's birthplace, Stratford-upon-Avon). The most common anti-Stratfordian claim is that William Shakespeare simply was not educated enough or from a high enough social class to have written plays overflowing with references to such a wide range of subjects like history, the classics, religion, and international culture. William Shakespeare was the son of a glove-maker, he only had a basic grade school education, and he never set foot outside of England—so how could he have produced plays of such sophistication and imagination? How could he have written in such detail about historical figures and events, or about different cultures and locations around Europe? According to anti-Stratfordians, the depth of knowledge contained in Shakespeare's plays suggests a well-traveled writer from a wealthy background with a university education, not a countryside writer like Shakespeare. But in fact, there is not much substance to such speculation, and most anti-Stratfordian arguments can be refuted with a little background about Shakespeare's time and upbringing.

First of all, those who doubt Shakespeare's authorship often point to his common birth and brief education as stumbling blocks to his writerly genius. Although it is true that Shakespeare did not come from a noble class, his father was a very *successful* glove-maker and his mother was from a very wealthy land owning family—so while Shakespeare may have had a country upbringing, he was certainly from a well-off family and would have been educated accordingly. Also, even though he did not attend university, grade school education in Shakespeare's time was actually quite rigorous and exposed students to classic drama through writers like Seneca and Ovid. It is not unreasonable to believe that Shakespeare received a very solid foundation in poetry and literature from his early schooling.

Next, anti-Stratfordians tend to question how Shakespeare could write so extensively about countries and cultures he had never visited before (for instance, several of his most famous works like *Romeo and Juliet* and *The Merchant of Venice* were set in Italy, on the opposite side of Europe!). But again, this criticism does not hold up under scrutiny. For one thing, Shakespeare was living in London, a bustling metropolis of international trade, the most populous city in England, and a political and cultural hub of Europe. In the daily crowds of people, Shakespeare would certainly have been able to meet travelers from other countries and hear firsthand accounts of life in their home country. And, in addition to the influx of information from world travelers, this was also the age of the printing press, a jump in technology that made it possible to print and circulate books much more easily than in the past. This also allowed for a freer flow of information across different countries, allowing people to read about life and ideas from throughout Europe. One needn't travel the continent in order to learn and write about its culture.

18. Which sentence contains the author's thesis?
    a. People who argue that William Shakespeare is not responsible for the plays attributed to his name are known as anti-Stratfordians.
    b. But in fact, there is not much substance to such speculation, and most anti-Stratfordian arguments can be refuted with a little background about Shakespeare's time and upbringing.
    c. It is not unreasonable to believe that Shakespeare received a very solid foundation in poetry and literature from his early schooling.
    d. Next, anti-Stratfordians tend to question how Shakespeare could write so extensively about countries and cultures he had never visited before.

19. In the first paragraph, "How could he have written in such detail about historical figures and events, or about different cultures and locations around Europe?" is an example of which of the following?
    a. Hyperbole
    b. Onomatopoeia
    c. Rhetorical question
    d. Appeal to authority

20. How does the author respond to the claim that Shakespeare was not well-educated because he did not attend university?
    a. By insisting upon Shakespeare's natural genius.
    b. By explaining grade school curriculum in Shakespeare's time.
    c. By comparing Shakespeare with other uneducated writers of his time.
    d. By pointing out that Shakespeare's wealthy parents probably paid for private tutors.

21. The word "bustling" in the third paragraph most nearly means which of the following?
    a. Busy
    b. Foreign
    c. Expensive
    d. Undeveloped

The next article is for questions 22-24.

The Myth of Head Heat Loss

It has recently been brought to my attention that most people believe that 75% of your body heat is lost through your head. I had certainly heard this before, and am not going to attempt to say I didn't believe it when I first heard it. It is natural to be gullible to anything said with enough authority. But the "fact" that the majority of your body heat is lost through your head is a lie.

Let me explain. Heat loss is proportional to surface area exposed. An elephant loses a great deal more heat than an anteater, because it has a much greater surface area than an anteater. Each cell has mitochondria that produce energy in the form of heat, and it takes a lot more energy to run an elephant than an anteater.

So, each part of your body loses its proportional amount of heat in accordance with its surface area. The human torso probably loses the most heat, though the legs lose a significant amount as well. Some people have asked, "Why does it feel so much warmer when you cover your head than when you don't?" Well, that's because your head, because it is not clothed, is losing a lot of heat while the clothing on the rest of your body provides insulation. If you went outside with a hat and pants but no shirt, not only would you look silly, but your heat loss would be significantly greater because so much more of you would be exposed. So, if given the choice to cover your chest or your head in the cold, choose the chest. It could save your life.

22. Why does the author compare elephants and anteaters?
    a. To express an opinion.
    b. To give an example that helps clarify the main point.
    c. To show the differences between them.
    d. To persuade why one is better than the other.

23. Which of the following best describes the tone of the passage?
    a. Harsh
    b. Angry
    c. Casual
    d. Indifferent

24. The author appeals to which branch of rhetoric to prove their case?
    a. Factual evidence
    b. Emotion
    c. Ethics and morals
    d. Author qualification

Directions for questions 25–34

Read the statement or passage and then choose the best answer to the question. Answer the question based on what is stated or implied in the statement or passage.

25. While scientists aren't entirely certain why tornadoes form, they have some clues into the process. Tornadoes are dangerous funnel clouds that occur during a large thunderstorm. When warm, humid air near the ground meets cold, dry air from above, a column of the warm air can be drawn up into the

clouds. Winds at different altitudes blowing at different speeds make the column of air rotate. As the spinning column of air picks up speed, a funnel cloud is formed. This funnel cloud moves rapidly and haphazardly. Rain and hail inside the cloud cause it to touch down, creating a tornado. Tornadoes move in a rapid and unpredictable pattern, making them extremely destructive and dangerous. Scientists continue to study tornadoes to improve radar detection and warning times.

The main purpose of this passage is to:
    a. Show why tornadoes are dangerous
    b. Explain how a tornado forms
    c. Compare thunderstorms to tornadoes
    d. Explain what to do in the event of a tornado

26. There are two major kinds of cameras on the market right now for amateur photographers. Camera enthusiasts can either purchase a digital single-lens reflex camera (DSLR) camera or a compact system camera (CSC). The main difference between a DSLR and a CSC is that the DSLR has a full-sized sensor, which means it fits in a much larger body. The CSC uses a mirrorless system, which makes for a lighter, smaller camera. While both take quality pictures, the DSLR generally has better picture quality due to the larger sensor. CSCs still take very good quality pictures and are more convenient to carry than a DSLR. This makes the CSC an ideal choice for the amateur photographer looking to step up from a point-and-shoot camera.

The main difference between the DSLR and CSC is:
    a. The picture quality is better in the DSLR.
    b. The CSC is less expensive than the DSLR.
    c. The DSLR is a better choice for amateur photographers.
    d. The DSLR's larger sensor makes it a bigger camera than the CSC.

27. When selecting a career path, it's important to explore the various options available. Many students entering college may shy away from a major because they don't know much about it. For example, many students won't opt for a career as an actuary, because they aren't exactly sure what it entails. They would be missing out on a career that is very lucrative and in high demand. Actuaries work in the insurance field and assess risks and premiums. The average salary of an actuary is $100,000 per year. Another career option students may avoid, due to lack of knowledge of the field, is a hospitalist. This is a physician that specializes in the care of patients in a hospital, as opposed to those seen in private practices. The average salary of a hospitalist is upwards of $200,000. It pays to do some digging and find out more about these lesser-known career fields.

An actuary is:
    a. A doctor who works in a hospital
    b. The same as a hospitalist
    c. An insurance agent who works in a hospital
    d. A person who assesses insurance risks and premiums

28. Many people are unsure of exactly how the digestive system works. Digestion begins in the mouth where teeth grind up food and saliva breaks it down, making it easier for the body to absorb. Next, the food moves to the esophagus, and it is pushed into the stomach. The stomach is where food is stored and broken down further by acids and digestive enzymes, preparing it for passage into the intestines. The small intestine is where the nutrients are taken from food and passed into the blood stream. Other

essential organs like the liver, gall bladder, and pancreas aid the stomach in breaking down food and absorbing nutrients. Finally, food waste is passed into the large intestine where it is eliminated by the body.

The purpose of this passage is to:
    a. Explain how the liver works.
    b. Show why it is important to eat healthy foods
    c. Explain how the digestive system works
    d. Show how nutrients are absorbed by the small intestine

29. Hard water occurs when rainwater mixes with minerals from rock and soil. Hard water has a high mineral count, including calcium and magnesium. The mineral deposits from hard water can stain hard surfaces in bathrooms and kitchens as well as clog pipes. Hard water can stain dishes, ruin clothes, and reduce the life of any appliances it touches, such as hot water heaters, washing machines, and humidifiers.

One solution is to install a water softener to reduce the mineral content of water, but this can be costly. Running vinegar through pipes and appliances and using vinegar to clean hard surfaces can also help with mineral deposits.

From this passage, it can be concluded that:
    a. Hard water can cause a lot of problems for homeowners.
    b. Calcium is good for pipes and hard surfaces.
    c. Water softeners are easy to install.
    d. Vinegar is the only solution to hard water problems.

30. Osteoporosis is a medical condition that occurs when the body loses bone or makes too little bone. This can lead to brittle, fragile bones that easily break. Bones are already porous, and when osteoporosis sets in, the spaces in bones become much larger, causing them to weaken. Both men and women can contract osteoporosis, though it is most common in women over age 50. Loss of bone can be silent and progressive, so it is important to be proactive in prevention of the disease.

The main purpose of this passage is to:
    a. Discuss some of the ways people contract osteoporosis
    b. Describe different treatment options for those with osteoporosis
    c. Explain how to prevent osteoporosis
    d. Define osteoporosis

31. Vacationers looking for a perfect experience should opt out of Disney parks and try a trip on Disney Cruise Lines. While a park offers rides, characters, and show experiences, it also includes long lines, often very hot weather, and enormous crowds. A Disney Cruise, on the other hand, is a relaxing, luxurious vacation that includes many of the same experiences as the parks, minus the crowds and lines. The cruise has top-notch food, maid service, water slides, multiple pools, Broadway-quality shows, and daily character experiences for kids. There are also many activities, such as bingo, trivia contests, and dance parties that can entertain guests of all ages. The cruise even stops at Disney's private island for a beach barbecue with characters, waterslides, and water sports. Those looking for the Disney experience without the hassle should book a Disney cruise.

The main purpose of this passage is to:
- a. Explain how to book a Disney cruise
- b. Show what Disney parks have to offer
- c. Show why Disney parks are expensive
- d. Compare Disney parks to the Disney cruise

32. Coaches of kids' sports teams are increasingly concerned about the behavior of parents at games. Parents are screaming and cursing at coaches, officials, players, and other parents. Physical fights have even broken out at games. Parents need to be reminded that coaches are volunteers, giving up their time and energy to help kids develop in their chosen sport. The goal of kids' sports teams is to learn and develop skills, but it's also to have fun. When parents are out of control at games and practices, it takes the fun out of the sport.

From this passage, it can be concluded that:
- a. Coaches are modeling good behavior for kids.
- b. Organized sports are not good for kids.
- c. Parents' behavior at their kids' games needs to change.
- d. Parents and coaches need to work together.

33. As summer approaches, drowning incidents will increase. Drowning happens very quickly and silently. Most people assume that drowning is easy to spot, but a person who is drowning doesn't make noise or wave his arms. Instead, he will have his head back and his mouth open, with just his face out of the water. A person who is truly in danger of drowning is not able to wave his arms in the air or move much at all. Recognizing these signs of drowning can prevent tragedy.

The main purpose of this passage is to:
- a. Explain the dangers of swimming
- b. Show how to identify the signs of drowning
- c. Explain how to be a lifeguard
- d. Compare the signs of drowning

34. Technology has been invading cars for the last several years, but there are some new high tech trends that are pretty amazing. It is now standard in many car models to have a rear-view camera, hands-free phone and text, and a touch screen digital display. Music can be streamed from a paired cell phone, and some displays can even be programmed with a personal photo. Sensors beep to indicate there is something in the driver's path when reversing and changing lanes. Rain-sensing windshield wipers and lights are automatic, leaving the driver with little to do but watch the road and enjoy the ride. The next wave of technology will include cars that automatically parallel park, and a self-driving car is on the horizon. These technological advances make it a good time to be a driver.

It can be concluded from this paragraph that:
- a. Technology will continue to influence how cars are made.
- b. Windshield wipers and lights are always automatic.
- c. It is standard to have a rear-view camera in all cars.
- d. Technology has reached its peak in cars.

Directions for questions 35–44

For the questions that follow, two underlined sentences are followed by a question or statement. Read the sentences, then choose the best answer to the question or the best completion of the statement.

35. The NBA draft process is based on a lottery system among the teams who did not make the playoffs in the previous season to determine draft order. Only the top three draft picks are determined by the lottery.

What does the *second sentence* do?
    a. It contradicts the first.
    b. It supports the first.
    c. It restates information from the first.
    d. It offers a solution.

36. While many people use multiple social media sites, Facebook remains the most popular with more than one billion users. Instagram is rising in popularity and, with 100 million users, is now the most-used social media site.

What does the *second sentence* do?
    a. It expands on the first.
    b. It contradicts the first.
    c. It supports the first.
    d. It proposes a solution.

37. There are eight different phases of the moon, from new moon to new moon. One of the eight different moon phases is first quarter, commonly called a half moon.

What does the *second sentence* do?
    a. It provides an example.
    b. It contradicts the first.
    c. It states an effect.
    d. It offers a solution.

38. The terror attacks of September 11, 2001 have had many lasting effects on the United States. The Department of Homeland Security was created in late September 2001 in response to the terror attacks and became an official cabinet-level department in November of 2002.

What does the *second sentence* do?
    a. It contradicts the first.
    b. It restates the information from the first.
    c. It states an effect.
    d. It makes a contrast.

39. Annuals are plants that complete the life cycle in a single growing season. Perennials are plants that complete the life cycle in many growing seasons, dying in the winter and coming back each spring.

What does the *second sentence* do?
    a. It makes a contrast.
    b. It disputes the first sentence.
    c. It provides an example.
    d. It states an effect.

40. Personal computers can be subject to viruses and malware, which can lead to slow performance, loss of files, and overheating. Antivirus software is often sold along with a new PC to protect against viruses and malware.

What does the *second sentence* do?
    a. It makes a contrast.
    b. It provides an example.
    c. It restates the information from the first.
    d. It offers a solution.

41. Many companies tout their chicken as cage-free because the chickens are not confined to small wire cages. However, cage-free chickens are often crammed into buildings with thousands of other birds and never go outside in their short lifetime.

What does the *second sentence* do?
    a. It offers a solution.
    b. It provides an example.
    c. It disputes the first sentence.
    d. It states an effect.

42. Common core standards do not include the instruction of cursive handwriting. The next generation of students will not be able to read or write cursive handwriting.

What does the *second sentence* do?
    a. It offers a solution.
    b. It states an effect.
    c. It contradicts the first sentence.
    d. It restates the first sentence.

43. Air travel has changed significantly in the last ten years. Airlines are now offering pay-as-you-go perks, including no baggage fees, seat selection, and food and drinks on the flight to keep costs low.

What does the *second sentence* do?
    a. It states effects.
    b. It provides examples.
    c. It disputes the first sentence.
    d. It offers solutions.

44. Many people are unaware that fragrances and other chemicals in their favorite products are causing skin reactions and allergies. Surprisingly, many popular products contain ingredients that can cause skin allergies.

What does the *second sentence* do?
    a. It restates the first sentence.
    b. It provides examples.
    c. It contradicts the first sentence.
    d. It provides solutions.

Answer Explanations

1. D: The passage directly states that the larger sensor is the main difference between the two cameras. Choices *A* and *B* may be true, but these answers do not identify the major difference between the two cameras. Choice *C* states the opposite of what the paragraph suggests is the best option for amateur photographers, so it is incorrect.

2. D: An actuary assesses risks and sets insurance premiums. While an actuary does work in insurance, the passage does not suggest that actuaries have any affiliation with hospitalists or working in a hospital, so all other choices are incorrect.

3. A: The passage focuses mainly on the problems of hard water. Choice *B* is incorrect because calcium is not good for pipes and hard surfaces. The passage does not say anything about whether water softeners are easy to install, so Choice *C* is incorrect. Choice *D* is also incorrect because the passage does offer other solutions besides vinegar.

4. C: The main point of this paragraph is that parents need to change their poor behavior at their kids' sporting events. Choice *A* is incorrect because the coaches' behavior is not mentioned in the paragraph. Choice *B* suggests that sports are bad for kids, when the paragraph is about parents' behavior, so it is incorrect. While Choice *D* may be true, it offers a specific solution to the problem, which the paragraph does not discuss.

5. B: The main point of this passage is to show how a tornado forms. Choice *A* is off base because while the passage does mention that tornadoes are dangerous, it is not the main focus of the passage. While thunderstorms are mentioned, they are not compared to tornadoes, so Choice *C* is incorrect. Choice *D* is incorrect because the passage does not discuss what to do in the event of a tornado.

6. C: The purpose of this passage is to explain how the digestive system works. Choice *A* focuses only on the liver, which is a small part of the process and not the focus of the paragraph. Choice *B* is off-track because the passage does not mention healthy foods. Choice *D* only focuses on one part of the digestive system.

7. D: The main point of this passage is to define osteoporosis. Choice *A* is incorrect because the passage does not list ways that people contract osteoporosis. Choice *B* is incorrect because the passage does not mention any treatment options. While the passage does briefly mention prevention, it does not explain how, so Choice *C* is incorrect.

8. D: The passage compares Disney cruises with Disney parks. It does not discuss how to book a cruise, so Choice *A* is incorrect. Choice *B* is incorrect because though the passage does mention some of the park attractions, it is not the main point. The passage does not mention the cost of either option, so Choice *C* is incorrect.

9. B: The point of this passage is to show what drowning looks like. Choice *A* is incorrect because while drowning is a danger of swimming, the passage doesn't include any other dangers. The passage is not intended for lifeguards specifically, but for a general audience, so Choice *C* is incorrect. There are a few signs of drowning, but the passage does not compare them; thus, *D* is incorrect.

10. B: The scientist and politician largely disagree, but the question asks for a point where the two are in agreement. The politician would not concur that burning fossil fuels causes global temperatures to rise; thus, Choice *A* is wrong. The politician also would not agree with Choice *C* suggesting that countries must revisit their energy policies. By inference from the given information, the scientist would likely not concur that earth's climate naturally goes through warming and cooling cycles; so Choice *D* is incorrect. However, both the scientist and politician would agree that global temperatures are increasing. The reason for this is in dispute. The politician thinks it is part of the earth's natural cycle; the scientist thinks it is from the burning of fossil fuels. However, both acknowledge an increase, so Choice *B* is the correct answer.

11. C: We are looking for an inference—a conclusion that is reached on the basis of evidence and reasoning—from the passage that will likely explain why the famous children's author did not achieve her usual success with the new genre (despite the book's acclaim). Choice *A* is wrong because the statement is false according to the passage. Choice *B* is wrong because, although the passage says the author has a graduate degree on the subject, it would be an unrealistic leap to infer that she is the foremost expert on Antebellum America. Choice *D* is wrong because there is nothing in the passage to lead us to infer that people generally prefer a children's series to historical fiction. In contrast, Choice *C* can be logically inferred since the passage speaks of the great success of the children's series and the declaration that the fame of the author's name causes the children's books to "fly off the shelves." Thus, she did not receive any bump from her name since she published the historical novel under a pseudonym, and Choice *C* is correct.

12. B: The author is clearly opposed to tobacco. He cites disease and deaths associated with smoking. He points to the monetary expense and aesthetic costs. Choice *A* is incorrect because alternatives to smoking are not even addressed in the passage. Choice *C* is incorrect because it does not summarize the passage but rather is just a premise. Choice *D* is incorrect because, while these statistics are a premise in the argument, they do not represent a summary of the piece. Choice *B* is the correct answer because it states the three critiques offered against tobacco and expresses the author's conclusion.

13. C: We are looking for something the author would agree with, so it will almost certainly be anti-smoking or an argument in favor of quitting smoking. Choice *A* is incorrect because the author does not speak against means of cessation. Choice *B* is incorrect because the author does not reference other substances, but does speak of how addictive nicotine, a drug in tobacco, is. *Choice D* is incorrect because the author certainly would not encourage reducing taxes to encourage a reduction of smoking costs, thereby helping smokers to continue the habit *Choice C* is correct because the author is definitely attempting to persuade smokers to quit smoking.

14. D: Here, we are looking for an opinion of the author's rather than a fact or statistic. Choice *A* is incorrect because quoting statistics from the Centers of Disease Control and Prevention is stating facts, not opinions. Choice *B* is incorrect because it expresses the fact that cigarettes sometimes cost more than a few gallons of gas. It would be an opinion if the author said that cigarettes were not affordable. Choice *C* is incorrect because yellow stains are a known possible adverse effect of smoking. Choice *D* is correct as an opinion because smell is subjective. Some people might like the smell of smoke, they might not have working olfactory senses, and/or some people might not find the smell of smoke akin to "pervasive nastiness," so this is the expression of an opinion. Thus, Choice *D* is the correct answer.

15. C: Choice *A* is incorrect because it describes facts: Leif Erikson was the son of Erik the Red and historians debate Leif's date of birth. These are not opinions. Choice *B* is incorrect; that Erikson called the land Vinland is a verifiable fact as is Choice *D* because he did contact the natives almost 500 years before Columbus. Choice *C* is the correct answer because it is the author's opinion that Erikson deserves more credit. That, in fact, is his conclusion in the piece, but another person could argue that Columbus or another explorer deserves more credit for opening up the New World to exploration. Rather than being an incontrovertible fact, it is a subjective value claim.

16. B: Choice *A* is incorrect because the author aims to go beyond describing Erikson as a mere legendary Viking. Choice *C* is incorrect because the author does not focus on Erikson's motivations, let alone name the spreading of Christianity as his primary objective. Choice *D* is incorrect because it is a premise that Erikson contacted the natives 500 years before Columbus, which is simply a part of supporting the author's conclusion. Choice *B* is correct because, as stated in the previous answer, it accurately identifies the author's statement that Erikson deserves more credit than he has received for being the first European to explore the New World.

17. D: Choice *A* is incorrect because the author never addresses the Vikings' state of mind or emotions. Choice *B* is incorrect because the author does not elaborate on Erikson's exile and whether he would have become an explorer if not for his banishment. Choice *C* is incorrect because there is not enough information to support this premise. It is unclear whether Erikson informed the King of Norway of his finding. Although it is true that the King did not send a follow-up expedition, he could have simply chosen not to expend the resources after receiving Erikson's news. It is not possible to logically infer whether Erikson told him. Choice *D* is correct because there are two examples—Leif Erikson's date of birth and what happened during the encounter with the natives—of historians having trouble pinning down important dates in Viking history.

18. B: But in fact, there is not much substance to such speculation, and most anti-Stratfordian arguments can be refuted with a little background about Shakespeare's time and upbringing. The thesis is a statement that contains the author's topic and main idea. The main purpose of this article is to use historical evidence to provide counterarguments to anti-Stratfordians. Choice *A* is simply a definition; Choice *C* is a supporting detail, not a main idea; and Choice *D* represents an idea of anti-Stratfordians, not the author's opinion.

19. C: It is an example of a rhetorical question. This requires readers to be familiar with different types of rhetorical devices. A rhetorical question is a question that is asked not to obtain an answer but to encourage readers to more deeply consider an issue.

20. B: By explaining grade school curriculum in Shakespeare's time. This question asks readers to refer to the organizational structure of the article and demonstrate understanding of how the author provides details to support their argument. This particular detail can be found in the second paragraph: "even though he did not attend university, grade school education in Shakespeare's time was actually quite rigorous."

21. A: It most closely means busy. This is a vocabulary question that can be answered using context clues. Other sentences in the paragraph describe London as "the most populous city in England" filled with "crowds of people," giving an image of a busy city full of people. Choice *B* is incorrect because London was in Shakespeare's home country, not a foreign one. Choice *C* is not mentioned in the passage. Choice *D* is not a good answer choice because the passage describes how London was a popular and important city, probably not an underdeveloped one.

22. B: Choice *B* is correct because the author is trying to demonstrate the main idea, which is that heat loss is proportional to surface area, and so they compare two animals with different surface areas to clarify the main point. Choice *A* is incorrect because the author uses elephants and anteaters to prove a point, that heat loss is proportional to surface area, not to express an opinion. Choice *C* is incorrect because though the author does use them to show differences, they do so in order to give examples that prove the above points, so Choice *C* is not the best answer. Choice *D* is incorrect because there is no language to indicate favoritism between the two animals.

23. C: Because of the way that the author addresses the reader, and also the colloquial language that the author uses (i.e., "let me explain," "so," "well," didn't," "you would look silly," etc.), *C* is the best answer because it has a much more casual tone than the usual informative article. *Choice A* may be a tempting choice because the author says the "fact" that most of one's heat is lost through their head is a "lie," and that someone who does not wear a shirt in the cold looks silly, but it only happens twice within all the diction of the passage and it does not give an overall tone of harshness. *B* is incorrect because again, while not necessarily nice, the language does not carry an angry charge. The author is clearly not indifferent to the subject because of the passionate language that they use, so *D* is incorrect.

24. A: The author gives logical examples and reasons in order to prove that most of one's heat is not lost through their head, therefore *A* is correct. *B* is incorrect because there is not much emotionally charged language in this selection, and even the small amount present is greatly outnumbered by the facts and evidence. *C* is incorrect because there is no mention of ethics or morals in this selection. *D* is incorrect because the author never qualifies himself as someone who has the authority to be writing on this topic.

25. B: The main point of this passage is to show how a tornado forms. Choice *A* is off base because while the passage does mention that tornadoes are dangerous, it is not the main focus of the passage. While thunderstorms are mentioned, they are not compared to tornadoes, so Choice *C* is incorrect. Choice *D* is incorrect because the passage does not discuss what to do in the event of a tornado.

26. D: The passage directly states that the larger sensor is the main difference between the two cameras. Choices *A* and *B* may be true, but these answers do not identify the major difference between the two cameras. Choice *C* states the opposite of what the paragraph suggests is the best option for amateur photographers, so it is incorrect.

27. D: An actuary assesses risks and sets insurance premiums. While an actuary does work in insurance, the passage does not suggest that actuaries have any affiliation with hospitalists or working in a hospital, so all other choices are incorrect.

28. C: The purpose of this passage is to explain how the digestive system works. Choice *A* focuses only on the liver, which is a small part of the process and not the focus of the paragraph. Choice *B* is off-track because the passage does not mention healthy foods. Choice *D* only focuses on one part of the digestive system.

29. A: The passage focuses mainly on the problems of hard water. Choice *B* is incorrect because calcium is not good for pipes and hard surfaces. The passage does not say anything about whether water softeners are easy to install, so *C* is incorrect. *D* is also incorrect because the passage does offer other solutions besides vinegar.

30. D: The main point of this passage is to define osteoporosis. Choice *A* is incorrect because the passage does not list ways that people contract osteoporosis. Choice *B* is incorrect because the passage does not mention any treatment options. While the passage does briefly mention prevention, it does not explain how, so Choice *C* is incorrect.

31. D: The passage compares Disney cruises with Disney parks. It does not discuss how to book a cruise, so Choice *A* is incorrect. Choice *B* is incorrect because though the passage does mention some of the park attractions, it is not the main point. The passage does not mention the cost of either option, so Choice *C* is incorrect.

32. C: The main point of this paragraph is that parents need to change their poor behavior at their kids' sporting events. Choice *A* is incorrect because the coaches' behavior is not mentioned in the paragraph. *B* suggests that sports are bad for kids, when the paragraph is about parents' behavior, so it is incorrect. While Choice *D* may be true, it offers a specific solution to the problem, which the paragraph does not discuss.

33. B: The point of this passage is to show what drowning looks like. Choice *A* is incorrect because while drowning is a danger of swimming, the passage doesn't include any other dangers. The passage is not intended for lifeguards specifically, but for a general audience, so Choice *C* is incorrect. There are a few signs of drowning, but the passage does not compare them; thus, Choice *D* is incorrect.

34. A: The passage discusses recent technological advances in cars and suggests that this trend will continue in the future with self-driving cars. Choice *B* and *C* are not true, so these are both incorrect. Choice *D* is also incorrect because the passage suggests continuing growth in technology, not a peak.

35. B: The information in the second sentence further explains the draft process and thus supports the first sentence. It does not contradict the first sentence, so *A* is incorrect. Choice *C* and *D* are incorrect because the second sentence does not restate or offer a solution to the first.

36. B: The first sentence identifies Facebook as the most popular social media site with 1 billion users. The second sentence states that Instagram only has 100 million users, but is the most used. This contradicts the original sentence, so all other answers are incorrect.

37. A: The first sentence states that there are eight phases to the moon cycle. The second sentence discusses first quarter, which is one of the phases of the moon. Therefore, the second sentence provides an example of the first sentence.

38. C: The first sentence discusses the effects of the terror attacks of September 11, 2001. The second sentence states that the Department of Homeland Security was created in response to the terror attacks, so it states an effect of the first sentence.

39. A: The first sentence describes the life cycle of annuals. The second sentence describes the life cycle of perennials, making a contrast between the way annuals grow and the way perennials grow.

40. D: The first sentence describes how viruses can affect a PC. The second sentence offers a solution to the problem of viruses and malware on a PC.

41. C: The first sentence describes cage-free chickens as not being confined to a cage, suggesting they are treated humanely. The second sentence disputes the first sentence, showing that cage-free chickens are inhumanely confined to a larger area with many other chickens, never seeing the outdoors.

42. B: The first sentence states that schools are no longer teaching cursive handwriting. The second sentence shows that as an effect of the first sentence, students will no longer be able to read or write cursive handwriting.

43. B: The first sentence states that air travel has changed in the last decade. The second sentence provides examples of the changes that have occurred.

44. A: The first sentence discusses how fragrances and other chemicals in products can cause skin reactions. The second sentence states that many products contain ingredients that cause skin allergies, restating the same information from the first sentence.

Mathematics

Arithmetic

Addition with Whole Numbers and Fractions

Addition combines two quantities together. With whole numbers, this is taking two sets of things and merging them into one, then counting the result. For example, 4 + 3 = 7. When adding numbers, the order does not matter: 3 + 4 = 7, also. Longer lists of whole numbers can also be added together. The result of adding numbers is called the *sum*.

With fractions, the number on top is the *numerator*, and the number on the bottom is the *denominator*. To add fractions, the denominator must be the same—a *common denominator*. To find a common denominator, the existing numbers on the bottom must be considered, and the lowest number they will both multiply into must be determined. Consider the following equation:

$$\frac{1}{3} + \frac{5}{6} = ?$$

The numbers 3 and 6 both multiply into 6. Three can be multiplied by 2, and 6 can be multiplied by 1. The top and bottom of each fraction must be multiplied by the same number. Then, the numerators are added together to get a new numerator. The following equation is the result:

$$\frac{1}{3} + \frac{5}{6} = \frac{2}{6} + \frac{5}{6} = \frac{7}{6}$$

Subtraction with Whole Numbers and Fractions

Subtraction is taking one quantity away from another, so it is the opposite of addition. The expression 4 − 3 means taking 3 away from 4. So, 4 − 3 = 1. In this case, the order matters, since it entails taking one quantity away from the other, rather than just putting two quantities together. The result of subtraction is also called the *difference*.

To subtract fractions, the denominator must be the same. Then, subtract the numerators together to get a new numerator. Here is an example:

$$\frac{1}{3} - \frac{5}{6} = \frac{2}{6} - \frac{5}{6} = \frac{-3}{6} = -\frac{1}{2}$$

Multiplication with Whole Numbers and Fractions

Multiplication is a kind of repeated addition. The expression 4×5 is taking four sets, each of them having five things in them, and putting them all together. That means $4 \times 5 = 5 + 5 + 5 + 5 = 20$. As with addition, the order of the numbers does not matter. The result of a multiplication problem is called the *product*.

To multiply fractions, the numerators are multiplied to get the new numerator, and the denominators are multiplied to get the new denominator:

$$\frac{1}{3} \times \frac{5}{6} = \frac{1 \times 5}{3 \times 6} = \frac{5}{18}$$

When multiplying fractions, common factors can *cancel* or *divide into one another*, when factors that appear in the numerator of one fraction and the denominator of the other fraction. Here is an example:

$$\frac{1}{3} \times \frac{9}{8} = \frac{1}{1} \times \frac{3}{8} = 1 \times \frac{3}{8} = \frac{3}{8}$$

The numbers 3 and 9 have a common factor of 3, so that factor can be divided out.

Division with Whole Numbers and Fractions

Division is the opposite of multiplication. With whole numbers, it means splitting up one number into sets of equal size. For example, $16 \div 8$ is the number of sets of eight things that can be made out of sixteen things. Thus, $16 \div 8 = 2$. As with subtraction, the order of the numbers will make a difference, here. The answer to a division problem is called the *quotient*, while the number in front of the division sign is called the *dividend* and the number behind the division sign is called the *divisor*.

To divide fractions, the first fraction must be multiplied with the reciprocal of the second fraction. The *reciprocal* of the fraction $\frac{x}{y}$ is the fraction $\frac{y}{x}$. Here is an example:

$$\frac{1}{3} \div \frac{5}{6} = \frac{1}{3} \times \frac{6}{5} = \frac{6}{15} = \frac{2}{5}$$

Recognizing Equivalent Fractions and Mixed Numbers

The value of a fraction does not change if multiplying or dividing both the numerator and the denominator by the same number (other than 0). In other words, $\frac{x}{y} = \frac{a \times x}{a \times y} = \frac{x \div a}{y \div a}$, as long as a is not 0. This means that $\frac{2}{5} = \frac{4}{10}$, for example. If x and y are integers that have no common factors, then the fraction is said to be *simplified*. This means $\frac{2}{5}$ is simplified, but $\frac{4}{10}$ is not.

Often when working with fractions, the fractions need to be rewritten so that they all share a single denominator—this is called finding a *common denominator* for the fractions. Using two fractions, $\frac{a}{b}$ and $\frac{c}{d}$, the numerator and denominator of the left fraction can be multiplied by d, while the numerator and denominator of the right fraction can be multiplied by b. This provides the fractions $\frac{a \times d}{b \times d}$ and $\frac{c \times b}{d \times b}$ with the common denominator $b \times d$.

A fraction whose numerator is smaller than its denominator is called a *proper fraction*. A fraction whose numerator is bigger than its denominator is called an *improper fraction*. These numbers can be rewritten as a combination of integers and fractions, called a *mixed number*. For example, $\frac{6}{5} = \frac{5}{5} + \frac{1}{5} = 1 + \frac{1}{5}$, and can be written as $1\frac{1}{5}$.

Estimating

Estimation is finding a value that is close to a solution but is not the exact answer. For example, if there are values in the thousands to be multiplied, then each value can be estimated to the nearest thousand and the calculation performed. This value provides an approximate solution that can be determined very quickly.

Recognition of Decimals

The *decimal system* is a way of writing out numbers that uses ten different numerals: 0, 1, 2, 3, 4, 5, 6, 7, 8, and 9. This is also called a "base ten" or "base 10" system. Other bases are also used. For example, computers work with a base of 2. This means they only use the numerals 0 and 1.

The *decimal place* denotes how far to the right of the decimal point a numeral is. The first digit to the right of the decimal point is in the *tenths* place. The next is the *hundredths*. The third is the *thousandths*.

So, 3.142 has a 1 in the tenths place, a 4 in the hundredths place, and a 2 in the thousandths place.

The *decimal point* is a period used to separate the *ones* place from the *tenths* place when writing out a number as a decimal.

A *decimal number* is a number written out with a decimal point instead of as a fraction, for example, 1.25 instead of $\frac{5}{4}$. Depending on the situation, it can sometimes be easier to work with fractions and sometimes easier to work with decimal numbers.

A decimal number is *terminating* if it stops at some point. It is called *repeating* if it never stops, but repeats a pattern over and over. It is important to note that every rational number can be written as a terminating decimal or as a repeating decimal.

Addition with Decimals

To add decimal numbers, each number in columns needs to be lined up by the decimal point. For each number being added, the zeros to the right of the last number need to be filled in so that each of the numbers has the same number of places to the right of the decimal. Then, the columns can be added together. Here is an example of 2.45 + 1.3 + 8.891 written in column form:

$$2.450$$

$$1.300$$

$$+\ 8.891$$

Zeros have been added in the columns so that each number has the same number of places to the right of the decimal.

Added together, the correct answer is 12.641:

$$2.450$$

$$1.300$$

$$+\ 8.891$$

$$12.641$$

Subtraction with Decimals

Subtracting decimal numbers is the same process as adding decimals. Here is 7.89 – 4.235 written in column form:

$$7.890$$

$$-\ 4.235$$

$$3.655$$

A zero has been added in the column so that each number has the same number of places to the right of the decimal.

Multiplication with Decimals

Decimals can be multiplied as if there were no decimals points in the problem. For example, 0.5 x 1.25 can be rewritten and multiplied as 5 x 125, which equals 625.

The final answer will have the same number of decimal *points* as the total number of decimal *places* in the problem. The first number has one decimal place, and the second number has two decimal places. Therefore, the final answer will contain three decimal places:

0.5 x 1.25 = 0.625

Division with Decimals

Dividing a decimal by a whole number entails using long division first by ignoring the decimal point. Then, the decimal point is moved the number of places given in the problem.

For example, $6.8 \div 4$ can be rewritten as $68 \div 4$, which is 17. There is one non-zero integer to the right of the decimal point, so the final solution would have one decimal place to the right of the solution. In this case, the solution is 1.7.

Dividing a decimal by another decimal requires changing the divisor to a whole number by moving its decimal point. The decimal place of the dividend should be moved by the same number of places as the divisor. Then, the problem is the same as dividing a decimal by a whole number.

For example, $5.72 \div 1.1$ has a divisor with one decimal point in the denominator. The expression can be rewritten as $57.2 \div 11$ by moving each number one decimal place to the right to eliminate the decimal.

The long division can be completed as $572 \div 11$ with a result of 52. Since there is one non-zero integer to the right of the decimal point in the problem, the final solution is 5.2.

In another example, $8 \div 0.16$ has a divisor with two decimal points in the denominator. The expression can be rewritten as $800 \div 16$ by moving each number two decimal places to the right to eliminate the decimal in the divisor. The long division can be completed with a result of 50.

Fraction and Percent Equivalencies

The word *percent* comes from the Latin phrase for "per one hundred." A *percent* is a way of writing out a fraction. It is a fraction with a denominator of 100. Thus, $65\% = \frac{65}{100}$.

To convert a fraction to a percent, the denominator is written as 100. For example, $\frac{3}{5} = \frac{60}{100} = 60\%$.

In converting a percent to a fraction, the percent is written with a denominator of 100, and the result is simplified. For example, $30\% = \frac{30}{100} = \frac{3}{10}$.

Percent Problems

The basic percent equation is the following:

$$\frac{is}{of} = \frac{\%}{100}$$

The placement of numbers in the equation depends on what the question asks.

<u>Example 1</u>
Find 40% of 80.

Basically, the problem is asking, "What is 40% of 80?" The 40% is the percent, and 80 is the number to find the percent "of." The equation is:

$$\frac{x}{80} = \frac{40}{100}$$

Solving the equation by cross-multiplication, the problem becomes 100x = 80(40). Solving for x gives the answer: x = 32.

<u>Example 2</u>
What percent of 100 is 20?

The 20 fills in the "is" portion, while 100 fills in the "of." The question asks for the percent, so that will be x, the unknown. The following equation is set up:

$$\frac{20}{100} = \frac{x}{100}$$

Cross-multiplying yields the equation 100x = 20(100). Solving for x gives the answer of 20%.

Example 3
30% of what number is 30?

The following equation uses the clues and numbers in the problem:

$$\frac{30}{x} = \frac{30}{100}$$

Cross-multiplying results in the equation 30(100) = 30x. Solving for x gives the answer x = 100.

Problems Involving Estimation

Sometimes when multiplying numbers, the result can be estimated by *rounding*. For example, to estimate the value of 11.2×2.01, each number can be rounded to the nearest integer. This will yield a result of 22.

Rate, Percent, and Measurement Problems

A *ratio* compares the size of one group to the size of another. For example, there may be a room with 4 tables and 24 chairs. The ratio of tables to chairs is 4: 24. Such ratios behave like fractions in that both sides of the ratio by the same number can be multiplied or divided. Thus, the ratio 4:24 is the same as the ratio 2:12 and 1:6.

One quantity is *proportional* to another quantity if the first quantity is always some multiple of the second. For instance, the distance travelled in five hours is always five times to the speed as travelled. The distance is proportional to speed in this case.

One quantity is *inversely proportional* to another quantity if the first quantity is equal to some number divided by the second quantity. The time it takes to travel one hundred miles will be given by 100 divided by the speed travelled. The time is inversely proportional to the speed.

When dealing with word problems, there is no fixed series of steps to follow, but there are some general guidelines to use. It is important that the quantity that to be found is identified. Then, it can be determined how the given values can be used and manipulated to find the final answer.

Example 1
Jana wants to travel to visit Alice, who lives one hundred and fifty miles away. If she can drive at fifty miles per hour, how long will her trip take?

The quantity to find is the *time* of the trip. The time of a trip is given by the distance to travel divided by the speed to be traveled. The problem determines that the distance is one hundred and fifty miles, while the speed is fifty miles per hour. Thus, 150 divided by 50 is $150 \div 50 = 3$. Because *miles* and *miles per hour* are the units being divided, the miles cancel out. The result is 3 hours.

Example 2
Bernard wishes to paint a wall that measures twenty feet wide by eight feet high. It costs ten cents to paint one square foot. How much money will Bernard need for paint?

The final quantity to compute is the *cost* to paint the wall. This will be ten cents ($0.10) for each square foot of area needed to paint. The area to be painted is unknown, but the dimensions of the wall are given; thus, it can be calculated.

The dimensions of the wall are 20 feet wide and 8 feet high. Since the area of a rectangle is length multiplied by width, the area of the wall is 8 x 20 = 160 square feet. Multiplying 0.1 x 160 yields $16 as the cost of the paint.

The *average* or *mean* of a collection of numbers is given by adding those numbers together and then dividing by the total number of values. A *weighted average* or *weighted mean* is given by adding the numbers multiplied by their weights, then dividing by the sum of the weights:

$$\frac{w_1 x_1 + w_2 x_2 + w_3 x_3 \dots + w_n x_n}{w_1 + w_2 + w_3 + \dots + w_n}$$

An *ordinary average* is a weighted average where all the weights are 1.

Simple Geometry Problems

There are many key facts related to geometry that are applicable. The sum of the measures of the angles of a triangle are 180°, and for a quadrilateral, the sum is 360°. Rectangles and squares each have four right angles. A *right angle* has a measure of 90°.

Perimeter

The *perimeter* is the distance around a figure or the sum of all sides of a polygon.

The *formula for the perimeter of a square* is four times the length of a side. For example, the following square has side lengths of 8 feet:

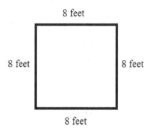

The perimeter is 32 feet because 4 times 8 is 32.

The *formula for a perimeter of a rectangle* is the sum of twice the length and twice the width. For example, if the length of a rectangle is 10 inches and the width 8 inches, then the perimeter is 36 inches because $P = 2l + 2w = 2(10) + 2(8) = 20 + 16 = 36$ inches.

Area

The area is the amount of space inside of a figure, and there are formulas associated with area.

The area of a triangle is the product of one-half the base and height. For example, if the base of the triangle is 2 feet and the height 4 feet, then the area is 4 square feet. The following equation shows the formula used to calculate the area of the triangle:

$$A = \frac{1}{2}bh = \frac{1}{2}(2)(4) = 4 \text{ square feet}$$

The area of a square is the length of a side squared, and the area of a rectangle is length multiplied by the width. For example, if the length of the square is 7 centimeters, then the area is 49 square centimeters. The formula for this example is $A = s^2 = 7^2 = 49$ square centimeters. An example of a rectangle is if the rectangle has a length of 6 inches and a width of 7 inches, then the area is 42 square inches:

$$A = lw = 6(7) = 42 \text{ square inches}$$

The area of a trapezoid is one-half the height times the sum of the bases. For example, if the length of the bases are 2.5 and 3 feet and the height 3.5 feet, then the area is 9.625 square feet. The following formula shows how the area is calculated:

$$A = \frac{1}{2}h(b_1 + b_2) = \frac{1}{2}(3.5)(2.5 + 3) = \frac{1}{2}(3.5)(5.5) = 9.625 \text{ square feet}$$

The perimeter of a figure is measured in single units, while the area is measured in square units.

Distribution of a Quantity into its Fractional Parts

A quantity may be broken into its fractional parts. For example, a toy box holds three types of toys for kids. $\frac{1}{3}$ of the toys are Type A and $\frac{1}{4}$ of the toys are Type B. With that information, how many Type C toys are there?

First, the sum of Type A and Type B must be determined by finding a common denominator to add the fractions. The lowest common multiple is 12, so that is what will be used. The sum is $\frac{1}{3} + \frac{1}{4} = \frac{4}{12} + \frac{3}{12} = \frac{7}{12}$.

This value is subtracted from 1 to find the number of Type C toys. The value is subtracted from 1 because 1 represents a whole. The calculation is $1 - \frac{7}{12} = \frac{12}{12} - \frac{7}{12} = \frac{5}{12}$. This means that $\frac{5}{12}$ of the toys are Type C. To check the answer, add all fractions together, and the result should be 1.

Practice Questions

1. 3.4+2.35+4=
    a. 5.35
    b. 9.2
    c. 9.75
    d. 10.25

2. $5.88 \times 3.2 =$
    a. 18.816
    b. 16.44
    c. 20.352
    d. 17

3. $\frac{3}{25} =$
    a. 0.15
    b. 0.1
    c. 0.9
    d. 0.12

4. Which of the following is largest?
    a. 0.45
    b. 0.096
    c. 0.3
    d. 0.313

5. Which of the following is NOT a way to write 40 percent of N?
    a. $(0.4)N$
    b. $\frac{2}{5}N$
    c. $40N$
    d. $\frac{4N}{10}$

6. Which is closest to 17.8×9.9?
    a. 140
    b. 180
    c. 200
    d. 350

7. A student gets an 85% on a test with 20 questions. How many answers did the student solve correctly?
    a. 15
    b. 16
    c. 17
    d. 18

8. Four people split a bill. The first person pays for $\frac{1}{5}$, the second person pays for $\frac{1}{4}$, and the third person pays for $\frac{1}{3}$. What fraction of the bill does the fourth person pay?

    a. $\frac{13}{60}$

    b. $\frac{47}{60}$

    c. $\frac{1}{4}$

    d. $\frac{4}{15}$

9. 6 is 30% of what number?

    a. 18

    b. 20

    c. 24

    d. 26

10. $3\frac{2}{3} - 1\frac{4}{5} =$

    a. $1\frac{13}{15}$

    b. $\frac{14}{15}$

    c. $2\frac{2}{3}$

    d. $\frac{4}{5}$

11. What is $\frac{420}{98}$ rounded to the nearest integer?

    a. 4

    b. 3

    c. 5

    d. 6

12. $4\frac{1}{3} + 3\frac{3}{4} =$

    a. $6\frac{5}{12}$

    b. $8\frac{1}{12}$

    c. $8\frac{2}{3}$

    d. $7\frac{7}{12}$

13. Five of six numbers have a sum of 25. The average of all six numbers is 6. What is the sixth number?

    a. 8

    b. 10

    c. 11

    d. 12

14. $52.3 \times 10^{-3} =$
    a. 0.00523
    b. 0.0523
    c. 0.523
    d. 523

15. If $\frac{5}{2} \div \frac{1}{3} = n$, then n is between:
    a. 5 and 7
    b. 7 and 9
    c. 9 and 11
    d. 3 and 5

16. A closet is filled with red, blue, and green shirts. If $\frac{1}{3}$ of the shirts are green and $\frac{2}{5}$ are red, what fraction of the shirts are blue?
    a. $\frac{4}{15}$
    b. $\frac{1}{5}$
    c. $\frac{7}{15}$
    d. $\frac{1}{2}$

17. Shawna buys $2\frac{1}{2}$ gallons of paint. If she uses $\frac{1}{3}$ of it on the first day, how much does she have left?
    a. $1\frac{5}{6}$ gallons
    b. $1\frac{1}{2}$ gallons
    c. $1\frac{2}{3}$ gallons
    d. 2 gallons

Answer Explanations

1. C: The decimal points are lined up, with zeroes put in as needed. Then, the numbers are added just like integers:

$$
\begin{array}{r}
3.40 \\
2.35 \\
+4.00 \\
\hline
9.75
\end{array}
$$

2. A: This problem can be multiplied as 588×32, except at the end, the decimal point needs to be moved three places to the left. Performing the multiplication will give 18,816, and moving the decimal place over three places results in 18.816.

3. D: The fraction is converted so that the denominator is 100 by multiplying the numerator and denominator by 4, to get $\frac{3}{25} = \frac{12}{100}$. Dividing a number by 100 just moves the decimal point two places to the left, with a result of 0.12.

4. A: Figure out which is largest by looking at the first non-zero digits. Choice *B*'s first non-zero digit is in the hundredths place. The other three all have non-zero digits in the tenths place, so it must be *A*, *C*, or *D*. Of these, *A* has the largest first non-zero digit.

5. C: $40N$ would be 4000% of *N*. It's possible to check that each of the others is actually 40% of *N*.

6. B: Instead of multiplying these out, the product can be estimated by using $18 \times 10 = 180$. The error here should be lower than 15, since it is rounded to the nearest integer, and the numbers add to something less than 30.

7. C: 85% of a number means multiplying that number by 0.85. So, $0.85 \times 20 = \frac{85}{100} \times \frac{20}{1}$, which can be simplified to $\frac{17}{20} \times \frac{20}{1} = 17$.

8. A: To find the fraction of the bill that the first three people pay, the fractions need to be added, which means finding common denominator. The common denominator will be 60. $\frac{1}{5} + \frac{1}{4} + \frac{1}{3} = \frac{12}{60} + \frac{15}{60} + \frac{20}{60} = \frac{47}{60}$. The remainder of the bill is $1 - \frac{47}{60} = \frac{60}{60} - \frac{47}{60} = \frac{13}{60}$.

9. B: 30% is 3/10. The number itself must be 10/3 of 6, or $\frac{10}{3} \times 6 = 10 \times 2 = 20$.

10. A: These numbers to improper fractions: $\frac{11}{3} - \frac{9}{5}$. Take 15 as a common denominator: $\frac{11}{3} - \frac{9}{5} = : \frac{55}{15} - \frac{27}{15} = \frac{28}{15} = 1\frac{13}{15}$ (when rewritten to get rid of the partial fraction).

11. B: Dividing by 98 can be approximated by dividing by 100, which would mean shifting the decimal point of the numerator to the left by 2. The result is 4.2 and rounds to 3.

12. B: $4\frac{1}{3} + 3\frac{3}{4} = 4 + 3 + \frac{1}{3} + \frac{3}{4} = 7 + \frac{1}{3} + \frac{3}{4}$. Adding the fractions gives $\frac{1}{3} + \frac{3}{4} = \frac{4}{12} + \frac{9}{12} = \frac{13}{12} = 1 + \frac{1}{12}$. Thus, $7 + \frac{1}{3} + \frac{3}{4} = 7 + 1 + \frac{1}{12} = 8\frac{1}{12}$.

13. C: The average is calculated by adding all six numbers, then dividing by 6. The first five numbers have a sum of 25. If the total divided by 6 is equal to 6, then the total itself must be 36. The sixth number must be $36 - 25 = 11$.

14. B: Multiplying by 10^{-3} means moving the decimal point three places to the left, putting in zeroes as necessary.

15. B: $\frac{5}{2} \div \frac{1}{3} = \frac{5}{2} \times \frac{3}{1} = \frac{15}{2} = 7.5$.

16. A: The total fraction taken up by green and red shirts will be $\frac{1}{3} + \frac{2}{5} = \frac{5}{15} + \frac{6}{15} = \frac{11}{15}$. The remaining fraction is $1 - \frac{11}{15} = \frac{15}{15} - \frac{11}{15} = \frac{4}{15}$.

17. C: If she has used 1/3 of the paint, she has 2/3 remaining. $2\frac{1}{2}$ gallons are the same as $\frac{5}{2}$ gallons. The calculation is $\frac{2}{3} \times \frac{5}{2} = \frac{5}{3} = 1\frac{2}{3}$ gallons.

Verbal Reasoning

Verbal Skills

To prepare for the Corrections Exam, it's helpful to review the parts of speech to see how they collectively function to form complete sentences (sentences with a subject and a predicate, also called *independent clauses*). Familiarity with parts of speech strengthens one's ability to fill in the blanks of the Cloze exercise correctly.

The Eight Parts of Speech		
Nouns	refer to people, places, things, or ideas	*mother, school, book, beauty*
Pronouns	alternatives for nouns	*I, you, she, it, this*
Verbs	express action or states of being	*run, drive, appear, remember*
Adjectives	modify nouns	*dark blue, average*
Adverbs	modify verbs; answer *when? where? how?* and *why?*	*soon, there, happily, entirely*
Prepositions	express the relationship between a noun and another element	*about, before, through, after*
Coordinating conjunctions	used to connect clauses or sentences or to coordinate words in the same clause	*and, but, for, yet, nor, so*
Interjections	exclamations	*Wow! Hi!*

Nouns

A *noun* is a word used to describe a person, place, thing, or idea. They are often the subject, object, or direct object of a sentence. There are five main types of nouns:

- Common nouns
- Proper nouns
- General nouns
- Specific nouns
- Collective nouns

Common nouns are general words that can be used to name people, places, and things:

- People: mom, brother, neighbor
- Places: office, gym, restaurant
- Things: bed, computer, sandwich

Proper nouns are specific words that can be used to name people, places, and things. For example:

- People: Amelia Earhart, Albert Einstein, Stephen Hawking
- Places: Philadelphia, Pennsylvania; Bombay, India; Australia
- Brands: Levi's jeans, Apple computer

Note the difference between common and proper nouns:

- Common noun: The suspect said that she'd eaten breakfast with her sister that morning.
- Proper noun: The suspect said that she'd eaten breakfast with Jane Lowe that morning.

Sometimes common and proper nouns appear in the same sentence:

George Washington was the first *president*.

General nouns are words used to describe conditions or ideas. They are abstract by nature. For example:

- Condition: bravery, love
- Idea: justice, freedom

Specific nouns are words used to describe particular people, places, and things. For example:

- People: victim, perpetrator, officer
- Places: city, beach, stadium
- Things: holster, badge, custody

Collective nouns are words used to refer to groups of people, places, or things as a whole. For example, *flock, group, bunch, crowd, tribe,* and *pack* are all collective nouns.

Pronouns

A *pronoun* is a word that replaces a noun in a sentence. There are seven types:

- Personal
- Reflexive
- Relative
- Interrogative
- Demonstrative
- Indefinite
- Reciprocal

Personal Pronouns
Personal pronouns are words that represent specific people or things (for example, I, you, he, she, me, you, and mine).

Three things must be considered in choosing the correct personal pronoun: *grammatical case, quantity,* and *point of view*.

Grammatical Case

A noun or pronoun's case refers to its relationship to the other words in a sentence. There are three cases of pronouns:

Nominative	nouns and pronouns that are the subject of a verb	I, we, you, he, she, it, they
Objective	nouns and pronouns that are the direct or indirect objects of a verb	Me, us, you, him, her, it, they
Possessive	used to show ownership	Me, mine, ours, your, yours, his, her, hers, its, their

Quantity

When referring to a quantity that is more than, the pronouns must be singular (I, him, you—one person). When referring to a quantity of more than one, the pronoun must be plural (we, their, your—several people).

Point of View

Point of view refers to perspective. There are three types of point of view:

First person refers to the perspective of the person speaking.

> *I* did not do anything.

Second person refers to the perspective of a person being spoken to.

> *You* are a witness.

Third person refers to the perspective of a person being spoken about.

> *The suspect* fled the vicinity.

Reflexive Pronouns

Reflexive pronouns are preceded by the adverb, adjective, pronoun, or noun to which they refer. They are used to rename the subjects of action verbs or function as different types of objects: *myself, himself, herself, themselves, yourself, yourselves, ourselves.*

> She was in a hurry, so she did the reports *herself*.

Intensive pronouns are reflexive pronouns that are only used to add *emphasis* to the subject of a sentence; they aren't required for meaning: *myself, yourself, himself, herself, itself, ourselves, yourselves,* and *themselves*.

> We met the king *himself*.

Relative Pronouns

Relative pronouns are used to connect phrases or clauses to a noun or pronoun. There are eight relative pronouns: *that, which, who, whom, whose, whichever, whoever,* and *whomever*.

> The first point of entry was closed, *which* meant we had to enter through the back.

Interrogative Pronouns

Interrogative pronouns are used to ask a question. There are five interrogative pronouns: *what, which, who, whom,* and *whose.*

>*Whose* boots are those?

Special note about *who/whom*: substitute *he* for *who* and *him* for *whom* to determine which should be used.

>[*Who* or *whom*] *wrote that email?*

>He wrote that email?

>Him wrote that email?

He=who, so *who* is correct.

>She gave the presentation to [*who* or *whom*]?

>She gave the presentation to he?

>She gave the presentation to him?

Him=whom, so *whom* is correct.

Demonstrative Pronouns

Demonstrative pronouns take the place of a noun phrase. There are six demonstrative pronouns: *this, that, these, those, none,* and *neither.*

>*That* is not the right thing to do.

Indefinite Pronouns

Indefinite pronouns are used when referring to a person or thing in a general way. Some examples *include all, another, any, anyone, each, everything, nobody,* and *several.*

>*Each* is separated by category.

Reciprocal Pronouns

Reciprocal pronouns are used when two or more people have done something simultaneously. The two reciprocal pronouns are: *each other* and *one another.*

>They were kind to *each other.*

Verbs

Verbs are words that express actions or occurrences; they signal the sentence's predicate (what the subject is doing). While a noun is often the subject of a sentence, the verb expresses what is happening or what has happened. For a sentence to be complete, a verb must be included. There are three main types of verbs: *action, linking,* and *helping.*

Action Verbs

Action verbs are verbs that show that something is happening, or that something/someone is in possession of something else.

Security personnel *detained* the prisoner.

Detective Suarez *has* a subject in custody.

There are two types of action verbs: transitive and intransitive.

Transitive verbs refer to an object that is receiving the action. There must be a direct object.

The sergeant apprehended the suspect.

The transitive verb in this sentence is *apprehended*. *The suspect* is the verb's direct object, that is, that which receives the action. Without the direct object to go along with the transitive verb, the sentence wouldn't make sense: *the sergeant apprehended.* Transitive verbs can be active or passive:

A verb is *active* if the subject of the sentence performs the action. Transitive active verbs are the verbs in sentences with direct objects.

Officer Lee *pursued* the suspect.

The subject, *Officer Lee*, performed the action, *pursued*, and *the suspect* is the direct object that receives that action.

The verb is *passive* if the subject or direct object is on the receiving end of the action.

The suspect *was pursued* by Officer Lee.

In this sentence, the subject of the sentence is *the suspect* and it is receiving Officer Lee's action.

Intransitive verbs are action words that don't need direct objects.

The recruits progressed well.

The verb in this sentence is *progressed*. We know it is an intransitive verb because a direct object (what they progressed in or with) is unnecessary for the sentence to be complete.

Linking Verbs

Linking verbs are verbs that link the subject of the sentence to more information about that subject.

The altercation *was* verbal.

In this sentence, *the altercation* is the subject, and we learn something new about it—*what kind* of altercation it was. *Was* serves as the verb in this sentence, linking the subject and the added information.

Common Linking Verbs			
is	are	seems	feels
was	become	might	am

Some action verbs can also be linking verbs.

> The defendant *appeared* before the court.

In the sentence above, *appeared* is an action verb.

> The defendant *appeared remorseful* when addressing the judge.

In the sentence above, *appeared* links the defendant to the subject complement, *remorseful.*

Helping Verbs

Helping verbs are words that appear before action or linking verbs. Their purpose is to add information about either time or possibility. The addition of a helping verb to an action or linking verb creates a verb phrase.

> Andrew *is appearing* before the judge.

In this sentence, *Andrew* is the subject, *is* is the helping verb, and *appearing* is the action verb.

Common Helping Verbs			
am	is	are	was
were	be	being	been
have	has	had	do
does	did	done	could
should	would	can	might

Conjugation

Conjugation refers to changing verbs to indicate *point of view, number, tense,* and *mood.* It also refers to subject/verb agreement.

Point of View

Verbs are conjugated to match the point of view of the subject of a sentence.

> I *am* a police officer.

In this sentence, *am* is a conjugation of the verb *to be*, for the subject *I*. *I to be a police officer*, or *I are a police officer,* are incorrect.

<u>Number</u>
Verbs are conjugated to indicate how many people are involved in the action of a sentence.

> *She runs* a ten-minute mile.

> *They run* every day.

The verb *to run* is conjugated by adding an *s* to indicate that one person is running. If the action includes more than one person, the conjugation changes: an *s* is not needed.

<u>Tense</u>
The tense of a verb indicates when the action is taking place. There are six possible verb tenses:

- Present: The action is currently happening or happens habitually.
- Past: The action has happened already.
- Future: The action will happen at a later date.
- Present perfect: The action started in the past and continues.
- Past perfect: Two actions occurred in the past, one before the other.
- Future perfect: The action will be complete before another action occurs in the future.

Conjugating a verb so that it is in the present or past tense is as simple as changing the form through letter addition or substitution. For the other tenses, including future, present perfect, past perfect, and future perfect, a helping verb is required.

Present: I run.	*Present perfect*: I have run.
Past: I ran.	*Past perfect*: I had run.
Future: I will run.	*Future perfect*: I will have run.

<u>Mood</u>
The *mood* indicates the purpose of a sentence and the speaker's general attitude. There are five common moods:

- Indicative: used for facts, opinions, and questions.

  > The officer wrote a ticket. ← This is a statement of fact.

- Imperative: used for orders and requests.

  > Put your hands on the vehicle. ← This is an order.

- Interrogative: used for questioning.

  > Will you stand down? ← This is a question.

- Conditional: used in a "what if" conditional state that will cause something else to happen.

    I might break my arm if I slip on the ice. ← This is a "what if" causal scenario.

- Subjunctive: used for wishes and other statements that are doubtful or not factual.

    I wish that no one used drugs. ← This expresses a wish.

Voice

The voice of a verb is active if the subject of the sentence is performing the action. If the subject is on the receiving end of the action, the verb is passive. See also *transitive verbs*.

Adjectives

An *adjective* is a word used to modify or describe a noun or pronoun. By answering questions about the noun or pronoun, adjectives make a sentence more specific. An adjective usually answers one of three questions:

- Which one?

    The *older* brother was seen entering the building.

    In this sentence, the *brother* is the subject. The adjective, *older*, tells us which one.

- What kind?

    Professional officers can become detectives.

    In this sentence, the adjective, *professional,* tells us what kind of officer can become a detective.

- How many or how often?

    She drinks milk *five* times a day.

    In this sentence, the adjective, *five*, tells us how many times a day the person drinks milk.

Articles

Another type of adjective is an *article*, which is used to identify a noun in a sentence. There are three articles in the English language: *the, a,* and *an. The* is a *definite* article, and *a* and *an* are *indefinite* articles, so it's important to choose the right one for meaning.

The is used when there is a limited number (definite) of something being referred to.

    I left *the book* on the couch.

In this sentence, the noun being referred to is *book*. Choosing the article *the* indicates that one particular book was left on the couch.

A and *an* are used when there is not a fixed amount (indefinite) of something being referred to.

> I left *a book* on the couch.

Again, the noun in the sentence is *book*. The article changed to *a* because the sentence no longer refers to one specific book.

On the Cloze Test, it will be important to remember that *an* comes before nouns that begin with a vowel.

> I left *an old* book on the couch.

Comparisons

Adjectives can also be used to make comparisons. These adjectives come in two forms: relative and absolute.

Relative adjectives show a comparison between two things. There are three degrees of relative adjectives: *positive*, *comparative*, and *superlative*.

- Positive: the base form of the adjective

  > The painting was *beautiful.*

- *Comparative*: a higher level of some quality of the adjective

  > The painting was *more* beautiful than I expected it to be.

- *Superlative*: The highest form of quality of the adjective

  > The painting was the *most beautiful* painting I've ever seen.

Absolute adjectives also show comparison, but not in varying degrees; they're *non-gradable.* A good example of an absolute adjective is *empty.* If there are two boxes, and one of them is *empty*, the other box cannot be *emptier, more emptier,* or *most empty.* The box is either empty or it is not. *Empty* is an absolute adjective.

Adverbs

An *adverb* is a word or phrase that modifies verbs, adjectives, or other adverbs. Like adjectives, adverbs are also words that can be used to answer questions. Adverbs answer the following:

- When? She drove *yesterday.*
- Where? They drove *here.*
- How? He drove *quickly.*
- To what extent? She drives *whenever possible.*
- Why? We ride the bus *to avoid traffic.*

As seen in the examples, some adverbs end in *–ly*, but not all. The words *not* and *never* are considered adverbs because they modify adjectives.

Again, like adjectives, adverbs can be used to make comparisons in three degrees: *positive, comparative,* and *superlative.*

- They *quietly* went into the building.
- The squad went into the building *more quietly* than the cadets.
- The squad leader went into the building *most quietly.*

Prepositions

A *preposition* is a word that appears in a sentence to show the relationship between a noun or pronoun and another element.

> The books are *on* the shelves.

The preposition, *on*, shows the relationship between the books (noun) and the shelves (another noun).

Common Prepositions				
aboard	behind	during	outside	to
about	below	for	over	toward
above	beyond	inside	past	under
among	by	into	since	upon
around	despite	near	through	within

Conjunctions

Conjunctions join pieces of words, phrases, or clauses. There are three types of conjunctions: *coordinating, correlative,* and *subordinating.*

Coordinating Conjunctions
Coordinating conjunctions connect equal parts of sentences. Common coordinating conjunctions are *for, and, nor, but, or, yet, so* (sometimes called the FANBOYS).

> The poem was brief, *but* it was beautiful.

In this sentence *but* connects two independent clauses into one sentence.

In some cases, coordinating conjunctions convey a sense of contrast. In the example above, the poem's beauty is in contrast to the length of it.

Correlative Conjunctions
Correlative conjunctions show the connection between pairs. Common correlative conjunctions are *either/or, neither/nor, not only/but also, both/and, whether/or,* and *so/as.*

> *Either* you're having lunch at home, *or* you're eating out.

In this sentence, *either* and *or* are used to connect two options.

Subordinating Conjunctions

Subordinating conjunctions join dependent clauses with independent clauses, providing a transition between two ideas. This transition often adds information about time, place, or the effect of something.

Our team lost the game *because* Jim was unprepared.

In this sentence, *because* is connecting two clauses and indicating a cause and effect relationship between them.

Common Subordinating Conjunctions		
after	since	whenever
although	so that	where
because	unless	wherever
before	when	in order that

Interjections

An *interjection* is an exclamatory word used to indicate extreme emotion or feeling. Some examples include *Hey! Oh!* and *Wow!*

These words can be used alone as a complete sentence, or they can be added to a sentence to indicate a forceful change in thought or add feeling.

Wow! You look great today!

Hey, in my opinion, he deserves the presidency.

In the first sentence, *Wow!* is the interjection used to add feeling to the speaker's opinion. In the second sentence, the speaker uses *Hey* to grab the listener's attention before expressing their opinion.

Types of Sentences

There isn't an overabundance of absolutes in grammar, but here is one: every sentence in the English language falls into one of four categories.

- Declarative: a simple statement that ends with a period

  The price of milk per gallon is the same as the price of gasoline.

- Imperative: a command, instruction, or request that ends with a period

  Buy milk when you stop to fill up your car with gas.

- Interrogative: a question that ends with a question mark

  Will you buy the milk?

- Exclamatory: a statement or command that expresses emotions like anger, urgency, or surprise and ends with an exclamation mark

  Buy the milk now!

Declarative sentences are the most common type, probably because they are comprised of the most general content, without any of the bells and whistles that the other three types contain. They are, simply, declarations or statements of any degree of seriousness, importance, or information.

Imperative sentences often seem to be missing a subject. The subject is there, though; it is just not visible or audible because it is *implied*. Look at the imperative example sentence.

> Buy the milk when you fill up your car with gas.

You is the implied subject, the one to whom the command is issued. This is sometimes called *the understood you* because it is understood that *you* is the subject of the sentence.

Interrogative sentences—those that ask questions—are defined as such from the idea of the word *interrogation*, the action of questions being asked of suspects by investigators. Although that is serious business, interrogative sentences apply to all kinds of questions.

To exclaim is at the root of *exclamatory* sentences. These are made with strong emotions behind them. The only technical difference between a declarative or imperative sentence and an exclamatory one is the exclamation mark at the end. The example declarative and imperative sentences can both become an exclamatory one simply by putting an exclamation mark at the end of the sentences.

> The price of milk per gallon is the same as the price of gasoline!
> Buy milk when you stop to fill up your car with gas!

After all, someone might be really excited by the price of gas or milk, or they could be mad at the person that will be buying the milk! However, as stated before, exclamation marks in abundance defeat their own purpose! After a while, they begin to cause fatigue! When used only for their intended purpose, they can have their expected and desired effect.

Subjects

Every sentence must include a subject and a verb. The *subject* of a sentence is who or what the sentence is about. It's often directly stated and can be determined by asking "Who?" or "What?" did the action:

Most sentences contain a direct subject, in which the subject is mentioned in the sentence.

> *Kelly mowed the lawn.*

> Who mowed the lawn? *Kelly*

> *The air-conditioner ran all night*

> What ran all night? *the air-conditioner*

The subject of imperative sentences is *you*, because imperative subjects are commands. the subject is implied because it is a command:

> *Go home after the meeting.*

> Who should go home after the meeting? *you* (implied)

In *expletive sentences* that start with "there are" or "there is," the subject is found after the predicate. The subject cannot be "there," so it must be another word in the sentence:

> *There is a cup sitting on the coffee table.*

> What is sitting on the coffee table? *a cup*

Simple and Complete Subjects

A *complete subject* includes the simple subject and all the words modifying it, including articles and adjectives. A *simple subject* is the single noun without its modifiers.

> A warm, chocolate-chip cookie sat on the kitchen table.

> Complete subject: *a warm, chocolate-chip cookie*

> Simple subject: *cookie*

The words *a, warm, chocolate,* and *chip* all modify the simple subject *cookie*.

There might also be a *compound subject*, which would be two or more nouns without the modifiers.

> A little girl and her mother walked into the shop.

> Complete subject: *A little girl and her mother*

> Compound subject: *girl, mother*

In this case, *the girl and her mother* are both completing the action of walking into the shop, so this is a *compound subject*.

Predicates

In addition to the subject, a sentence must also have a predicate. The *predicate* contains a verb and tells something about the subject. In addition to the verb, a predicate can also contain a direct or indirect object, object of a preposition, and other phrases.

> The cats napped on the front porch.

In this sentence, *cats* is the subject because they are who or what the sentence is about.

The *complete predicate* is everything else in the sentence: *napped on the front porch.* This phrase is the predicate because it tells us what the cats did.

This sentence can be broken down into a simple subject and predicate:

> Cats napped.

In this sentence, *cats* is the simple subject, and *napped* is the *simple predicate*.

Although the sentence is very short and doesn't offer much information, it's still considered a complete sentence because it contains a subject and predicate.

Like a compound subject, a sentence can also have a **compound predicate**. This is when the subject is or does two or more things in the sentence.

This easy chair reclines and swivels.

In this sentence, *this easy chair* is the complete subject. *Reclines and swivels* shows two actions of the chair, so this is the compound predicate.

Subject-Verb Agreement

The subject of a sentence and its verb must agree. The cornerstone rule of subject-verb agreement is that subject and verb must agree in number. Whether the subject is singular or plural, the verb must follow suit.

Incorrect: The houses is new.
Correct: The houses are new.
Also Correct: The house is new.

In other words, a singular subject requires a singular verb; a plural subject requires a plural verb. The words or phrases that come between the subject and verb do not alter this rule.

Incorrect: The houses built of brick is new.
Correct: The houses built of brick are new.

Incorrect: The houses with the sturdy porches is new.
Correct: The houses with the sturdy porches are new.

The subject will always follow the verb when a sentence begins with *here* or *there.* Identify these with care.

Incorrect: Here *is* the *houses* with sturdy porches.
Correct: Here *are* the *houses* with sturdy porches.

The subject in the sentences above is not *here*, it is *houses*. Remember, *here* and *there* are never subjects. Be careful that contractions such as *here's* or *there're* do not cause confusion!

Two subjects joined by *and* require a plural verb form, except when the two combine to make one thing:

Incorrect: Garrett and Jonathan is over there.
Correct: Garrett and Jonathan are over there.

Incorrect: Spaghetti and meatballs are a delicious meal!
Correct: Spaghetti and meatballs is a delicious meal!

In the example above, *spaghetti and meatballs* is a compound noun. However, *Garrett and Jonathan* is not a compound noun.

Two singular subjects joined by *or, either/or,* or *neither/nor* call for a singular verb form.

> Incorrect: Butter or syrup are acceptable.
> Correct: Butter or syrup is acceptable.

Plural subjects joined by *or, either/or,* or *neither/nor* are, indeed, plural.

> The chairs or the boxes are being moved next.

If one subject is singular and the other is plural, the verb should agree with the closest noun.

> Correct: The chair or the boxes are being moved next.
> Correct: The chairs or the box is being moved next.

Some plurals of money, distance, and time call for a singular verb.

> Incorrect: Three dollars *are* enough to buy that.
> Correct: Three dollars *is* enough to buy that.

For words declaring degrees of quantity such as *many of, some of,* or *most of,* let the noun that follows *of* be the guide:.

> Incorrect: Many of the books is in the shelf.
> Correct: Many of the books are in the shelf.

> Incorrect: Most of the pie *are* on the table.
> Correct: Most of the pie *is* on the table.

For indefinite pronouns like anybody or everybody, use singular verbs.

> Everybody *is* going to the store.

However, the pronouns *few, many, several, all, some,* and *both* have their own rules and use plural forms.

> Some *are* ready.

Some nouns like *crowd* and *congress* are called *collective nouns* and they require a singular verb form.

> Congress *is* in session.
> The news *is* over.

Books and movie titles, though, including plural nouns such as *Great Expectations*, also require a singular verb. Remember that only the subject affects the verb. While writing tricky subject-verb arrangements, say them aloud. Listen to them. Once the rules have been learned, one's ear will become sensitive to them, making it easier to pick out what's right and what's wrong.

Direct Objects

The *direct object* is the part of the sentence that receives the action of the verb. It is a noun and can usually be found after the verb. To find the direct object, first find the verb, and then ask the question *who* or *what* after it.

> The bear climbed the tree.

> What did the bear climb? *the tree*

Indirect Objects

An *indirect object* receives the direct object. It is usually found between the verb and the direct object. A strategy for identifying the indirect object is to find the verb and ask the questions *to whom/for whom* or *to what/ for what*.

> Jane made her daughter a cake.

> For whom did Jane make the cake? *her daughter*

Cake is the direct object because it is what Jane made, and *daughter* is the indirect object because she receives the cake.

Complements

A *complement* completes the meaning of an expression. A complement can be a pronoun, noun, or adjective. A verb complement refers to the direct object or indirect object in the sentence. An object complement gives more information about the direct object:

> The magician got the kids excited.

> *Kids* is the direct object, and *excited* is the object complement.

A *subject complement* comes after a linking verb. It is typically an adjective or noun that gives more information about the subject:

> The king was noble and spared the thief's life.

Noble describes the *king* and follows the linking verb *was*.

Predicate Nouns

A *predicate noun* renames the subject:

> John is a carpenter.

The subject is *John*, and the predicate noun is *carpenter*.

Predicate Adjectives

A *predicate adjective* describes the subject:

> Margaret is beautiful.

The subject is *Margaret*, and the predicate adjective is *beautiful*.

Homonyms

Homonyms are words that sound the same but are spelled differently, and they have different meanings. There are several common homonyms that give writers trouble.

There, They're, and *Their*
The word *there* can be used as an adverb, adjective, or pronoun:

> *There* are ten children on the swim team this summer.

> I put my book over *there*, but now I can't find it.

The word *they're* is a contraction of the words *they* and *are*:

> *They're* flying in from Texas on Tuesday.

The word *their* is a possessive pronoun:

> I store *their* winter clothes in the attic.

Its and *It's*
Its is a possessive pronoun:

> The cat licked *its* injured paw.

It's is the contraction for the words *it* and *is*:

> *It's* unbelievable how many people opted not to vote in the last election.

Your and You're
Your is a possessive pronoun:

> Can I borrow *your* lawnmower this weekend?

You're is a contraction for the words *you* and *are*:

> *You're* about to embark on a fantastic journey.

To, Too, and *Two*
To is an adverb or a preposition used to show direction, relationship, or purpose:

> We are going *to* New York.

> They are going *to* see a show.

Too is an adverb that means more than enough, also, and very:

You have had *too* much candy.

We are on vacation that week, *too*.

Two is the written-out form of the numeral 2:

Two of the shirts didn't fit, so I will have to return them.

New and Knew

New is an adjective that means recent:

There's a *new* customer on the phone.

Knew is the past tense of the verb *know*:

I *knew* you'd have fun on this ride.

Affect and Effect

Affect and *effect* are complicated because they are used as both nouns and verbs, have similar meanings, and are pronounced the same.

	Affect	Effect
Noun Definition	emotional state	result
Noun Example	The patient's affect was flat.	The effects of smoking are well documented.
Verb Definition	to influence	to bring about
Verb Example	The pollen count affects my allergies.	The new candidate hopes to effect change.

Independent and Dependent Clauses

Independent and *dependent* clauses are strings of words that contain both a subject and a verb. An independent clause *can* stand alone as complete thought, but a dependent clause *cannot*. A dependent clause relies on other words to be a complete sentence.

Independent clause: The keys are on the counter.
Dependent clause: If the keys are on the counter

Notice that both clauses have a subject (*keys*) and a verb (*are*). The independent clause expresses a complete thought, but the word *if* at the beginning of the dependent clause makes it *dependent* on other words to be a complete thought.

Independent clause: If the keys are on the counter, please give them to me.

This presents a complete sentence since it includes at least one verb and one subject and is a complete thought. In this case, the independent clause has two subjects (*keys* & an implied *you*) and two verbs (*are* & *give*).

Independent clause: I went to the store.
Dependent clause: Because we are out of milk,

Complete Sentence: Because we are out of milk, I went to the store.

Complete Sentence: I went to the store because we are out of milk.

Phrases

A *phrase* is a group of words that do not make a complete thought or a clause. They are parts of sentences or clauses. Phrases can be used as nouns, adjectives, or adverbs. A phrase does not contain both a subject and a verb.

Prepositional Phrases

A *prepositional phrase* shows the relationship between a word in the sentence and the object of the preposition. The object of the preposition is a noun that follows the preposition.

> The orange pillows are on the couch.

On is the preposition, and *couch* is the object of the preposition.

> She brought her friend with the nice car.

With is the preposition, and *car* is the object of the preposition. Here are some common prepositions:

about	as	at	after
by	for	from	in
of	on	to	with

Verbals and Verbal Phrases

Verbals are forms of verbs that act as other parts of speech. They can be used as nouns, adjectives, or adverbs. Though they are use verb forms, they are not to be used as the verb in the sentence. A word group that is based on a verbal is considered a *verbal phrase*. There are three major types of verbals: *participles, gerunds,* and *infinitives.*

Participles are verbals that act as adjectives. The present participle ends in *–ing,* and the past participle ends in *–d, -ed, -n,* or-*t.*

Verb	Present Participle	Past Participle
walk	walking	walked
share	sharing	shared

Participial phrases are made up of the participle and modifiers, complements, or objects.

> Crying for most of an hour, the baby didn't seem to want to nap.

> Having already taken this course, the student was bored during class.

> *Crying for most of an hour* and *Having already taken this course* are the participial phrases.

Gerunds are verbals that are used as nouns and end in –*ing*. A gerund can be the subject or object of the sentence like a noun. Note that a present participle can also end in –*ing*, so it is important to distinguish between the two. The gerund is used as a noun, while the participle is used as an adjective.

Swimming is my favorite sport.

I wish I were sleeping.

A *gerund phrase* includes the gerund and any modifiers or complements, direct objects, indirect objects, or pronouns.

Cleaning the house is my least favorite weekend activity.

Cleaning the house is the gerund phrase acting as the subject of the sentence.

The most important goal this year is raising money for charity.

Raising money for charity is the gerund phrase acting as the direct object.

The police accused the woman of stealing the car.

The *gerund* phrase *stealing the car* is the object of the preposition in this sentence.

An *infinitive* is a verbal made up of the word to and a verb. Infinitives can be used as nouns, adjectives, or adverbs.

Examples: To eat, to jump, to swim, to lie, to call, to work

An *infinitive phrase* is made up of the infinitive plus any complements or modifiers. The infinitive phrase *to wait* is used as the subject in this sentence:

To wait was not what I had in mind.

The infinitive phrase *to sing* is used as the subject complement in this sentence:

Her dream is to sing.

The infinitive phrase *to grow* is used as an adverb in this sentence:

Children must eat to grow.

Appositive Phrases

An *appositive* is a noun or noun phrase that renames a noun that comes immediately before it in the sentence. An appositive can be a single word or several words. These phrases can be *essential* or *nonessential*. An essential appositive phrase is necessary to the meaning of the sentence and a nonessential appositive phrase is not. It is important to be able to distinguish these for purposes of comma use.

Essential: My sister Christina works at a school.

Naming which sister is essential to the meaning of the sentence, so no commas are needed.

>Nonessential: My sister, who is a teacher, is coming over for dinner tonight.

Who is a teacher is not essential to the meaning of the sentence, so commas are required.

Absolute Phrases

An *absolute phrase* modifies a noun without using a conjunction. It is not the subject of the sentence and is not a complete thought on its own. Absolute phrases are set off from the independent clause with a comma.

>*Arms outstretched,* she yelled at the sky.

>*All things considered*, this has been a great day.

The Four Types of Sentence Structures

A *simple sentence* has one independent clause.

>I am going to win.

A *compound sentence* has two independent clauses. A conjunction—*for, and, nor, but, or, yet, so*—links them together. Note that each of the independent clauses has a subject and a verb.

>I am going to win, but the odds are against me.

A *complex sentence* has one independent clause and one or more dependent clauses.

>I am going to win, even though I don't deserve it.

Even though I don't deserve it is a dependent clause. It does not stand on its own. Some conjunctions that link an independent and a dependent clause are *although, because, before, after, that, when, which*, and *while*.

A *compound-complex sentence* has at least three clauses, two of which are independent and at least one that is a dependent clause.

While trying to dance, I tripped over my partner's feet, but I regained my balance quickly.

>The dependent clause is *While trying to dance*.

Sentence Fragments

A *sentence fragment* is an incomplete sentence. An independent clause is made up of a subject and a predicate, and both are needed to make a complete sentence.

Sentence fragments are often begin with *relative pronouns* (when, which*), subordinating conjunctions (*because, although*) or *gerunds* (trying, being, seeing). They might be missing the subject or the predicate.

The most common type of fragment is the isolated dependent clause, which can be corrected by joining it to the independent clause that appears before or after the fragment:

Fragment: While the cookies baked.

Correction: While the cookies baked, we played cards. (We played cards while the cookies baked.)

Run-on Sentences

A *run-on sentence* is created when two independent clauses (complete thoughts) are joined without correct punctuation or a conjunction. Run-on sentences can be corrected in the following ways:

- Join the independent clauses with a comma and coordinating conjunction.

    Run-on: We forgot to return the library books we had to pay a fine.

    Correction: We forgot to return the library books, so we had to pay a fine.

- Join the independent clauses with a semicolon, dash, or colon when the clauses are closely related in meaning.

    Run-on: I had a salad for lunch every day this week I feel healthier already.

    Correction: I had a salad for lunch every day this week; I feel healthier already.

- Join the independent clauses with a *semicolon and a conjunctive adverb.*

    Run-on: We arrived at the animal shelter on time however the dog had already been adopted.

    Correction: We arrived at the animal shelter on time; however, the dog had already been adopted.

- Separate the independent clauses into two sentences *with a period.*

    Run-on: He tapes his favorite television show he never misses an episode.

    Correction: He tapes his favorite television show. He never misses an episode.

- *Rearrange the wording* of the sentence to create an independent clause and a dependent clause.

    Run-on: My wedding date is coming up I am getting more excited to walk down the aisle.

    Correction: As my wedding date approaches, I am getting more excited to walk down the aisle.

Dangling and Misplaced Modifiers

A *modifier* is a phrase that describes, alters, limits, or gives more information about a word in the sentence. The two most common issues are dangling and misplaced modifiers.

A *dangling modifier* is created when the phrase modifies a word that is not clearly stated in the sentence.

> Dangling modifier: Having finished dinner, the dishes were cleared from the table.

> Correction: Having finished dinner, Amy cleared the dishes from the table.

In the first sentence, *having finished dinner* appears to modify *the dishes*, which obviously can't finish dinner. The second sentence adds the subject *Amy*, to make it clear who has finished dinner.

> Dangling modifier: Hoping to improve test scores, all new books were ordered for the school.

> Correction: Hoping to improve test scores, administrators ordered all new books for the school.

> Without the subject *administrators*, it appears the books are hoping to improve test scores, which doesn't make sense.

Misplaced modifiers are placed incorrectly in the sentence, which can cause confusion. Compare these examples:

> Misplaced modifier: Rory purchased a new flat screen television and placed it on the wall above the fireplace, with all the bells and whistles.

> Revised: Rory purchased a new flat screen television, with all the bells and whistles, and placed it on the wall above the fireplace.

The bells and whistles should modify the television, not the fireplace.

> Misplaced modifier: The delivery driver arrived late with the pizza, who was usually on time.

> Revised: The delivery driver, who usually was on time, arrived late with the pizza.

This suggests that the delivery driver was usually on time, instead of the pizza.

> Misplaced modifier: We saw a family of ducks on the way to church.

> Revised: On the way to church, we saw a family of ducks.

> The misplaced modifier, here, suggests the *ducks* were on their way to church, instead of the pronoun *we*.

Split Infinitives

An infinitive is made up of the word *to* and a verb, such as: to run, to jump, to ask. A *split infinitive* is created when a word comes between *to* and the verb.

Split infinitive: To quickly run

Correction: To run quickly

Split infinitive: To quietly ask

Correction: To ask quietly

Double Negatives

A *double negative* is a negative statement that includes two negative elements. This is incorrect in Standard English.

Incorrect: She hasn't never come to my house to visit.

Correct: She has never come to my house to visit.

The intended meaning is that she has never come to the house, so the double negative is incorrect. However, it is possible to use two negatives to create a positive statement.

Correct: She was not unhappy with her performance on the quiz.

In this case, the double negative, *was not unhappy*, is intended to show a positive, so it is correct. This means that she was somewhat happy with her performance.

Faulty Parallelism

It is necessary to use parallel construction in sentences that have multiple similar ideas. Using parallel structure provides clarity in writing. *Faulty parallelism* is created when multiple ideas are joined using different sentence structures. Compare these examples:

Incorrect: We start each practice with stretches, a run, and fielding grounders.
Correct: We start each practice with stretching, running, and fielding grounders.

Incorrect: I watched some television, reading my book, and fell asleep.
Correct: I watched some television, read my book, and fell asleep.

Incorrect: *Some of the readiness skills for Kindergarten are to cut with scissors, to tie shoes, and dressing independently.*
Correct: *Some of the readiness skills for Kindergarten are being able to cut with scissors, to tie shoes, and to dress independently.*

Subordination

If multiple pieces of information in a sentence are not equal, they can be joined by creating an independent clause and a dependent clause. The less important information becomes the *subordinate clause*:

> Draft: The hotel was acceptable. We wouldn't stay at the hotel again.

> Revised: Though the hotel was acceptable, we wouldn't stay there again.

The more important information (*we wouldn't stay there again*) becomes the main clause, and the less important information (*the hotel was acceptable*) becomes the subordinate clause.

Context Clues

Context clues help readers understand unfamiliar words, and thankfully, there are many types.

Synonyms are words or phrases that have nearly, if not exactly, the same meaning as other words or phrases

> *Large* boxes are needed to pack *big* items.

Antonyms are words or phrases that have opposite definitions. Antonyms, like synonyms, can serve as context clues, although more cryptically.

> *Large* boxes are not needed to pack *small* items.

Definitions are sometimes included within a sentence to define uncommon words.

> They practiced the *rumba*, a *type of dance*, for hours on end.

Explanations provide context through elaboration.

> Large boxes holding items weighing over 60 pounds were stacked in the corner.

Here's an example of *contrast*:

> These *minute* creatures were much different than the *huge* mammals that the zoologist was accustomed to dealing with.

Agreement in Number

Subjects and verbs must agree in number. If a sentence has a singular subject, then it must use a singular verb. If there is a plural subject, then it must use a plural verb.

Singular Noun	Singular Verb	Plural Noun	Plural verb
Man	has	men	have
child	plays	children	play
basketball	bounces	basketballs	bounce

Agreement in Person

Verbs must also agree in person. A subject that uses first person must include a verb that is also in first person. The same is true for second and third person subjects and verbs.

	Noun	Verb
First person	I	am
Second person	you	are
Third person	she	is

Common Agreement Errors

Compound Subjects
Compound subjects are when two or more subjects are joined by a coordinating conjunction, such as *and*, *or*, *neither*, or *nor*. Errors in agreement sometimes occur when there is a compound subject:

Incorrect: Mike and I am in a meeting this morning.

Correct: Mike and I are in a meeting this morning.

A compound subject always uses the plural form of the verb to match with the plural subject. In the above example, readers can substitute "Mike and I" for "we" to make it easier to determine the verb: "We *are* in a meeting this morning."

Separation of Subject and Verb
Errors sometimes occur when the subject is separated from the verb by a prepositional phrase or parenthetical element:

Incorrect: The objective of the teachers are to help students learn.

Correct: The objective of the teachers is to help students learn.

The verb must agree with the singular subject *objective*, not the word *teachers*, which is the object of the preposition *of* and does not influence the subject. An easy way to determine if the subject and verb agree is to take out the middle preposition: "The objective *is* to help students learn."

Indefinite Pronouns
Indefinite pronouns refer to people or groups in a general way: *each, anyone, none, all, either, neither,* and *everyone*. Some indefinite pronouns are always singular, such as *each, everyone, someone,* and *everybody*, which affects verb choice:

Incorrect: Each of them are competing in the race.

Correct: Each of them is competing in the race.

While the word *them* can indicate that a plural verb is needed, the subject *each* is singular regardless of what it refers to, requiring the singular verb, *is*.

Other indefinite pronouns can be singular or plural, depending on what they are referring to, such as *anyone, all,* and *some.*

> Some of the orders are scheduled to arrive today.

Some refers to *orders*, which is plural, so the plural verb (*are*) is needed.

> Some of the cake is left on the dining room table.

Some refers to *cake*, which is singular, so the singular verb (*is*) is needed.

Subjects Joined by Or and Nor
Compound subjects joined by *or* or *nor* rely on the subject nearest to the verb to determine conjugation and agreement:

> Neither Ben nor Jeff was in attendance at the conference.

> Pink or purple is the bride's color choice.

In each example, the subjects are both singular, so the verb should be singular.

If one subject is singular and the other plural, the subject nearest to the verb is the one that needs to agree:

> Either the shirt or pants are hanging on the clothesline.

In this example there is a singular subject (*shirt*) and a plural subject (*pants*), so the verb (*are*) should agree with the subject nearest to it (*pants*).

Collective Nouns
Collective nouns can use a singular or plural verb depending on their function in the sentence. If the collective noun is acting as a unit, then a singular verb is needed. Otherwise, it's necessary to use a plural verb.

> The staff is required to meet every third Friday of the month.

The *staff* is meeting as a collective unit, so a singular verb is needed.

> The staff are getting in their cars to go home.

The staff get into their cars separately, so a plural verb is needed.

Plural Nouns with Singular Meaning
Certain nouns end in *s*, like a plural noun, but have singular meaning, such as *mathematics, news,* and *civics*. These nouns should use a singular verb.

> The news is on at 8:00 tonight.

Nouns that are single things, but have two parts, are considered plural and should use a plural verb, such as *scissors, pants,* and *tweezers.*

> My favorite pants are in the washing machine.

<u>There Is and There Are</u>

There cannot be a subject, so verb agreement should be based on a word that comes after the verb.

> There is a hole in the road.

The subject in this sentence is *hole*, which is singular, so the verb should be singular (*is*).

> There are kids playing kickball in the street.

The subject in this sentence is *kids*, which is plural, so the verb should be plural (*are*).

Verb Tense

Shifting verb forms entails conjugation, which is used to indicate tense, voice, or mood.

Verb tense is used to show when the action in the sentence took place. There are several different verb tenses, and it is important to know how and when to use them. Some verb tenses can be achieved by changing the form of the verb, while others require the use of helping verbs (e.g., *is, was,* or *has*).

- *Present tense* shows the action is happening currently or is ongoing:

  > I walk to work every morning.

  > She is stressed about the deadline.

- *Past tense* shows that the action happened in the past or that the state of being is in the past:

  > I walked to work yesterday morning.

  > She was stressed about the deadline.

- *Future tense* shows that the action will happen in the future or is a future state of being:

  > I will walk to work tomorrow morning.

  > She will be stressed about the deadline.

- *Present perfect tense* shows action that began in the past, but continues into the present:

  > I have walked to work all week.

  > She has been stressed about the deadline.

- *Past perfect tense* shows an action was finished before another took place:

  > I had walked all week until I sprained my ankle.

  > She had been stressed about the deadline until we talked about it.

- *Future perfect tense* shows an action that will be completed at some point in the future:

  > By the time the bus arrives, I will have walked to work already.

Sentence Structure

Sentence Types

There are four ways in which we can structure sentences: simple, compound, complex, and compound-complex. Sentences can be composed of just one clause or many clauses joined together.

When a sentence is composed of just one clause (an independent clause), we call it a simple sentence. Simple sentences do not necessarily have to be short sentences. They just require one independent clause with a subject and a predicate. For example:

Thomas marched over to Andrew's house.

Jonah and Mary constructed a simplified version of the Eiffel Tower with Legos.

When a sentence has two or more independent clauses we call it a compound sentence. The clauses are connected by a comma and a coordinating conjunction—*and, but, or, nor, for*—or by a semicolon. Compound sentences do not have dependent clauses. For example:

We went to the fireworks stand, and we bought enough fireworks to last all night.

The children sat on the grass, and then we lit the fireworks one at a time.

When a sentence has just one independent clause and includes one or more dependent clauses, we call it a complex sentence:

Because she slept well and drank coffee, Sarah was quite productive at work.

Although Will had coffee, he made mistakes while using the photocopier.

When a sentence has two or more independent clauses and at least one dependent clause, we call it a compound-complex sentence:

It may come as a surprise, but I found the tickets, and you can go to the show.

Jade is the girl who dove from the high-dive, and she stunned the audience silent.

Sentence Fragments

Remember that a complete sentence must have both a subject and a verb. Complete sentences consist of at least one independent clause. Incomplete sentences are called sentence fragments. A sentence fragment is a common error in writing. Sentence fragments can be independent clauses that start with subordinating words, such as *but, as, so that,* or *because,* or they could simply be missing a subject or verb.

You can correct a fragment error by adding the fragment to a nearby sentence or by adding or removing words to make it an independent clause. For example:

Dogs are my favorite animals. Because cats are too independent. (Incorrect; the word because creates a sentence fragment)

Dogs are my favorite animals because cats are too independent. (Correct; the fragment becomes a dependent clause.)

Dogs are my favorite animals. Cats are too independent. (Correct; the fragment becomes a simple sentence.)

Run-on Sentences

Another common mistake in writing is the run-on sentence. A run-on is created when two or more independent clauses are joined without the use of a conjunction, a semicolon, a colon, or a dash. We don't want to use commas where periods belong. Here is an example of a run-on sentence:

Making wedding cakes can take many hours I am very impatient, I want to see them completed right away.

There are a variety of ways to correct a run-on sentence. The method you choose will depend on the context of the sentence and how it fits with neighboring sentences:

Making wedding cakes can take many hours. I am very impatient. I want to see them completed right away. (Use periods to create more than one sentence.)

Making wedding cakes can take many hours; I am very impatient—I want to see them completed right away. (Correct the sentence using a semicolon, colon, or dash.)

Making wedding cakes can take many hours and I am very impatient, so I want to see them completed right away. (Correct the sentence using coordinating conjunctions.)

I am very impatient because I would rather see completed wedding cakes right away than wait for it to take many hours. (Correct the sentence by revising.)

Dangling and Misplaced Modifiers

A modifier is a word or phrase meant to describe or clarify another word in the sentence. When a sentence has a modifier but is missing the word it describes or clarifies, it's an error called a dangling modifier. We can fix the sentence by revising to include the word that is being modified. Consider the following examples with the modifier italicized:

Having walked five miles, this bench will be the place to rest. (Incorrect; this version of the sentence implies that the bench walked the miles, not the person.)

Having walked five miles, Matt will rest on this bench. (Correct; in this version, *having walked five miles* correctly modifies *Matt,* who did the walking.)

Since midnight, my dreams have been pleasant and comforting. (Incorrect; in this version, the adverb clause *since midnight* cannot modify the noun *dreams*.)

Since midnight, I have had pleasant and comforting dreams. (Correct; in this version, *since midnight* modifies the verb *have had*, telling us when the dreams occurred.)

Sometimes the modifier is not located close enough to the word it modifies for the sentence to be clearly understood. In this case, we call the error a misplaced modifier. Here is an example with the modifier italicized and the modified word in underlined.

We gave the hot <u>cocoa</u> to the children *that was filled with marshmallows.* (Incorrect; this sentence implies that the children are what are filled with marshmallows.)

We gave the hot <u>*cocoa*</u> *that was filled with marshmallows* to the children. (Correct; here, the cocoa is filled with marshmallows. The modifier is near the word it modifies.)

Parallelism and Subordination

<u>Parallelism</u>
To be grammatically correct we must use articles, prepositions, infinitives, and introductory words for dependent clauses consistently throughout a sentence. This is called parallelism. We use parallelism when we are matching parts of speech, phrases, or clauses with another part of the sentence. Being inconsistent creates confusion. Consider the following example.

Incorrect: Be ready for running and to ride a bike during the triathlon.

Correct: Be ready to run and to ride a bike during the triathlon.

Correct: Be ready for running and for riding a bike during the triathlon.

In the incorrect example, the gerund *running* does not match with the infinitive *to ride*. Either both should be infinitives or both should be gerunds.

<u>Subordination</u>
Sometimes we have unequal pieces of information in a sentence where one piece is more important than the other. We need to show that one piece of information is subordinate to the other. We can make the more important piece an independent clause and connect the other piece by making it a dependent clause. Consider this example:

Central thought: Kittens can always find their mother.

Subordinate: Kittens are blind at birth.

Complex Sentence: Despite being blind at birth, kittens can always find their mother.

The sentence "Kittens are blind at birth" is made subordinate to the sentence "Kittens can always find their mother" by placing the word "Despite" at the beginning and removing the subject, thus turning an independent clause ("kittens are blind at birth") into a subordinate phrase ("Despite being blind at birth").

Sentence Logic

Clauses

Clauses are groups of words within a sentence that have both a subject and a verb. We can distinguish a clause from a phrase because phrases do not have both a subject and a verb. There are several types of clauses; clauses can be independent or dependent and can serve as a noun, an adjective, or an adverb.

An *independent clause* could stand alone as its own sentence if the rest of the sentence were not there. For example:

> *The party is on Tuesday* after the volleyball game is over.

> *I am excited to go to the party* because my best friend will be there.

A *dependent clause*, or subordinating clause, is the part of the sentence that gives supportive information but cannot create a proper sentence by itself. However, it will still have both a subject and a verb; otherwise, it is a phrase. In the example above, *after the volleyball game is over* and *because my best friend will be there* are dependent because they begin with the conjunctions *after* and *because*, and a proper sentence does not begin with a conjunction.

Noun clauses are groups of words that collectively form a noun. Look for the opening words *whether, which, what, that, who, how,* or *why.* For example:

> I had fun cooking *what we had for dinner last night.*

> I'm going to track down *whoever ate my sandwich.*

Adjective clauses collectively form an adjective that modifies a noun or pronoun in the sentence. If you can remove the adjective clause and the leftovers create a standalone sentence, then the clause should be set off with commas, parentheses, or dashes. If you can remove the clause it is called nonrestrictive. If it can't be removed without ruining the sentence then it is called restrictive and does not get set off with commas.

> Jenna, *who hates to get wet,* fell into the pool. (Nonrestrictive)

> The girl *who hates to get wet* fell into the pool. (Restrictive; the clause tells us which girl, and if removed there is confusion)

Adverbial clauses serve as an adverb in the sentence, modifying a verb, adjective, or other adverb. Look for the opening words *after, before, as, as if, although, because, if, since, so, so that, when, where, while,* or *unless.*

> She lost her wallet after she left the theme park.

> Her earring fell through the crack before she could catch it.

Phrases

A phrase is a group of words that go together but do not include both a subject and a verb. We use them to add information, explain something, or make the sentence easier for the reader to understand. Unlike clauses, phrases cannot ever stand alone as their own sentence if the rest of the sentence were not there. They do not form complete thoughts. There are noun phrases, prepositional phrases, verbal phrases, appositive phrases, and absolute phrases. Let's look at each of these.

Noun phrases: A noun phrase is a group of words built around a noun or pronoun that serves as a unit to form a noun in the sentence. Consider the following examples. The phrase is built around the underlined word. The entire phrase can be replaced by a noun or pronoun to test whether or not it is a noun phrase.

> I like the chocolate chip ice cream. (I like it.)

> I know all the shortest routes. (I know them.)

> I met the best supporting actress. (I met her.)

Prepositional phrases: These are phrases that begin with a preposition and end with a noun or pronoun. We use them as a unit to form the adjective or adverb in the sentence. Prepositional phrases that introduce a sentence are called introductory prepositional phrases and are set off with commas.

> I found the Frisbee *on the roof peak.* (Adverb; where it was found)

> The girl *with the bright red hair* was prom queen. (Adjective; which girl)

> *Before the sequel,* we wanted to watch the first movie. (Introductory phrase)

Verbal phrases: Some phrases look like verbs but do not serve as the verb in the sentence. These are called verbal phrases. There are three types: participial phrases, gerund phrases, and infinitive phrases.

Participial phrases start with a participle and modify nouns or pronouns; therefore, they act as the adjective in the sentence.

> *Beaten by the sun,* we searched for shade to sit in. (Modifies the pronoun *we*)

> The hikers, *being eaten by mosquitoes,* longed for repellant. (Modifies the noun *hikers*)

Gerund phrases often look like participles because they end in *-ing*, but they serve as the noun, not the adjective, in the sentence. Like any noun, we can use them as the subject or as the object of a verb or preposition in the sentence.

> *Eating green salad* is the best way to lose weight. (Subject)

> Sumo wrestlers are famous for *eating large quantities of food.* (Object)

Infinitive phrases often look like verbs because they start with the word *to,* but they serve as an adjective, adverb, or noun.

> *To survive the chill* is the goal of the Polar Bear Plunge. (Noun)

> A hot tub is at the scene *to warm up after the jump.* (Adverb)

> The jumpers have hot cocoa *to drink right away.* (Adjective)

Appositive phrases: We can use any of the above types of phrases to rename nouns or pronouns, and we call this an appositive phrase. Appositive phrases usually appear either just before or just after the noun or pronoun they are renaming. Appositive phrases are essential when the noun or pronoun is too general, and they are nonessential when they just add information.

The two famous brothers Orville and Wilbur Wright invented the airplane. (Essential)

Sarah Calysta, *my great grandmother,* is my namesake. (Nonessential)

Absolute phrases: When a participle comes after a noun and forms a phrase that is not otherwise part of the sentence, it's called an absolute phrase. Absolute phrases are not complete thoughts and cannot stand alone because they do not have a subject and a verb. They are not essential to the sentence in that they do not explain or add additional meaning to any other part of the sentence.

The engine roaring, Jada closed her eyes and waited for the plane to take off.

The microphone crackling, the flight attendant announced the delayed arrival.

Practice Questions

Read the selection and answer questions 1-5.

[1]I have to admit that when my father bought an RV, I thought he was making a huge mistake. [2]In fact, I even thought he might have gone a little bit crazy. [3]I did not really know anything about recreational vehicles, but I knew that my dad was as big a "city slicker" as there was. [4]On trips to the beach, he preferred to swim at the pool, and whenever he went hiking, he avoided touching any plants for fear that they might be poison ivy. [5]Why would this man, with an almost irrational fear of the outdoors, want a 40-foot camping behemoth?

[6]The RV was a great purchase for our family and brought us all closer together. [7]Every morning we would wake up, eat breakfast, and broke camp. [8]We laughed at our own comical attempts to back The Beast into spaces that seemed impossibly small. [9]We rejoiced when we figured out how to "hack" a solution to a nagging technological problem. [10]When things inevitably went wrong and we couldn't solve the problems on our own, we discovered the incredible helpfulness and friendliness of the RV community. We even made some new friends in the process.

[11] Above all, it allows us to share adventures travelling across America that we could not have experienced in cars and hotels. [12]Enjoying a campfire on a chilly summer evening with the mountains of Glacier National Park in the background, or waking up early in the morning to see the sun rising over the distant spires of Arches National Park are memories that will always stay with me and our entire family. [13]Those are also memories that my siblings and I have now shared with our own children.

1. How should the author change sentence 11?
   a. Above all, it will allow us to share adventures travelling across America that we could not have experienced in cars and hotels.
   b. Above all, it allows you to share adventures travelling across America that you could not have experienced in cars and hotels.
   c. Above all, it allowed us to share adventures travelling across America that we could not have experienced in cars and hotels.
   d. Above all, it allows them to share adventures travelling across America that they could not have experienced in cars and hotels.

2. Which of the following examples would make a good addition to the selection after sentence 4?
   a. My father is also afraid of seeing insects.
   b. My father is surprisingly good at starting a campfire.
   c. My father negotiated contracts for a living.
   d. My father isn't even bothered by pigeons.

3. Which of the following would correct the error in sentence 7?
   a. Every morning we would wake up, ate breakfast, and broke camp.
   b. Every morning we would wake up, eat breakfast, and broke camp.
   c. Every morning we would wake up, eat breakfast, and break camp.
   d. Every morning we would wake up, ate breakfast, and break camp.

4. What transition word could be added to the beginning of sentence 6?
   a. Not surprisingly,
   b. Furthermore,
   c. As it turns out,
   d. Of course,

5. Which of the following topics would fit well between paragraph 1 and paragraph 2?
   a. A guide to RV holding tanks
   b. Describing how RV travel is actually not as outdoors-oriented as many think
   c. A description of different types of RVs
   d. Some examples of how other RV enthusiasts helped the narrator and his father during their travels

6. Which of the following is a clearer way to describe the following phrase?
   "employee-manager relations improvement guide"
   a. A guide to employing better managers
   b. A guide to improving relations between managers and employees
   c. A relationship between employees, managers, and improvement
   d. An improvement in employees' and managers' use of guides

Read the sentences, and then answer the following question.

7. Polls show that more and more people in the US distrust the government and view it as dysfunctional and corrupt. Every election, the same people are voted back into office.

Which word or words would best link these sentences?
   a. Not surprisingly,
   b. Understandably,
   c. And yet,
   d. Therefore,

8. Which of the following statements would make the best conclusion to an essay about civil rights activist Rosa Parks?
   a. On December 1, 1955, Rosa Parks refused to give up her bus seat to a white passenger, setting in motion the Montgomery bus boycott.
   b. Rosa Parks was a hero to many, and came to symbolize the way that ordinary people could bring about real change in the Civil Rights Movement.
   c. Rosa Parks died in 2005 in Detroit, having moved from Montgomery shortly after the bus boycott.
   d. Rosa Parks' arrest was an early part of the Civil Rights Movement, and helped lead to the passage of the Civil Rights Act of 1964.

Select the best version of the underlined part of the sentence. If you think the original sentence is best, choose the first answer.

9. Since <u>none of the furniture were delivered</u> on time, we have to move in at a later date.
   a. none of the furniture were delivered
   b. none of the furniture was delivered
   c. all of the furniture were delivered
   d. all of the furniture was delivered

98

10. <u>An important issues stemming from this meeting</u> is that we won't have enough time to meet all of the objectives.

    a. An important issues stemming from this meeting

    b. Important issue stemming from this meeting

    c. An important issue stemming from this meeting

    d. Important issues stemming from this meeting

11. There were many questions <u>about what causes the case to have gone cold</u>, but the detective wasn't willing to discuss it with reporters.

    a. about what causes the case to have gone cold

    b. about why the case is cold

    c. about what causes the case to go cold

    d. about why the case went cold

Directions for questions 12-16: Select the best version of the underlined part of the sentence. The first choice is the same as the original sentence. If you think the original sentence is best, choose the first answer.

12. The fact <u>the train set only includes four cars and one small track was a big disappointment</u> to my son.

    a. the train set only includes four cars and one small track was a big disappointment

    b. that the trains set only include four cars and one small track was a big disappointment

    c. that the train set only includes four cars and one small track was a big disappointment

    d. that the train set only includes four cars and one small track were a big disappointment

13. The rising popularity of the clean eating movement can be attributed <u>to the fact that experts say added sugars and chemicals in our food are to blame for the obesity epidemic.</u>

    a. to the fact that experts say added sugars and chemicals in our food are to blame for the obesity epidemic.

    b. in the facts that experts say added sugars and chemicals in our food are to blame for the obesity epidemic.

    c. to the fact that experts saying added sugars and chemicals in our food are to blame for the obesity epidemic.

    d. with the facts that experts say added sugars and chemicals in our food are to blame for the obesity epidemic.

14. She's looking for a suitcase that can fit all of her <u>clothes, shoes, accessory, and makeup.</u>

    a. clothes, shoes, accessory, and makeup.

    b. clothes, shoes, accessories, and makeup.

    c. clothes, shoes, accessories, and makeups.

    d. clothes, shoe, accessory, and makeup.

15. <u>Because Shaun was used to playing guitar,</u> he needs to work much harder at playing bass.

    a. Because Shaun was used to playing guitar,

    b. Even though Shaun is used to playing guitar,

    c. While Shaun was used to playing guitar,

    d. Because Shaun is used to playing guitar,

16. <u>Considering the recent rains we have had, it's a wonder</u> the plants haven't drowned.
    a. Considering the recent rains we have had, it's a wonder
    b. Consider the recent rains we have had, it's a wonder
    c. Considering for how much recent rain we have had, it's a wonder
    d. Considering, the recent rains we have had, it's a wonder

Directions for questions 17-20: Rewrite the sentence in your head following the directions given below. Keep in mind that your new sentence should be well written and should have essentially the same meaning as the original sentence.

17. There are many risks in firefighting, including smoke inhalation, exposure to hazardous materials, and oxygen deprivation, so firefighters are outfitted with many items that could save their lives, including a self-contained breathing apparatus.

Rewrite, beginning with <u>so, firefighters.</u>

The next words will be which of the following?
    a. are exposed to lots of dangerous situations.
    b. need to be very careful on the job.
    c. wear life-saving protective gear.
    d. have very risky jobs.

18. Though social media sites like Facebook, Instagram, and Snapchat have become increasingly popular, experts warn that teen users are exposing themselves to many dangers such as cyberbullying and predators.

Rewrite, beginning with <u>experts warn that.</u>

The next words will be which of the following?
    a. Facebook is dangerous.
    b. they are growing in popularity.
    c. teens are using them too much.
    d. they can be dangerous for teens.

19. Student loan debt is at an all-time high, which is why many politicians are using this issue to gain the attention and votes of students, or anyone with student loan debt.

Rewrite, beginning with <u>Student loan debt is at an all-time high.</u>

The next words will be which of the following?
    a. because politicians want students' votes.
    b. , so politicians are using the issue to gain votes.
    c. , so voters are choosing politicians who care about this issue.
    d. , and politicians want to do something about it.

20. Seasoned runners often advise new runners to get fitted for better quality running shoes because new runners often complain about minor injuries like sore knees or shin splints.

Rewrite, beginning with <u>Seasoned runners often advise new runners to get fitted for better quality running shoes.</u>

The next words will be which of the following?
    a. to help them avoid minor injuries.
    b. because they know better.
    c. , so they can run further.
    d. to complain about running injuries.

Answer Explanations

1. C: The sentence should be in the same tense and person as the rest of the selection. The rest of the selection is in past tense and first person. Choice *A* is in future tense. Choice *B* is in second person. Choice *D* is in third person. While none of these sentences are incorrect by themselves, they are written in a tense that is different from the rest of the selection. Only *Choice C* maintains tense and voice consistent with the rest of the selection.

2. A: Choices *B* and *D* go against the point the author is trying to make—that the father is not comfortable in nature. Choice *C* is irrelevant to the topic. Choice *A* is the only choice that emphasizes the father's discomfort with spending time in nature.

3. C: This sentence uses verbs in a parallel series, so each verb must follow the same pattern. In order to fit with the helping verb "would," each verb must be in the present tense. In Choices *A*, *B*, and *D*, one or more of the verbs switches to past tense. Only Choice *C* remains in the same tense, maintaining the pattern.

4. C: In paragraph 2, the author surprises the reader by asserting that the opposite of what was expected was in fact true—the city slicker father actually enjoyed the RV experience. Only Choice *C* indicates this shift in expected outcome, while the other choices indicate a continuation of the previous expectation.

5. B: Choices *A* and *C* are irrelevant to the topic. They deal more with details about RVs while the author is more concerned with the family's experiences with them. Choice *D* is relevant to the topic, but it would fit better between paragraphs 2 and 3, since the author does not mention this point until the end of the second paragraph. Choice *B* would help explain to the reader why the father, who does not enjoy the outdoors, could end up enjoying RVs so much.

6. A: Stacked modifying nouns such as this example are untangled by starting from the end and adding words as necessary to provide meaning. In this case, a *guide* to *improving relations* between *managers* and *employees*. Choices *C* and *D* do not define the item first as a guide. Choice *A* does identify as a guide, but confuses the order of the remaining descriptors. Choice *B* is correct, as it unstacks the nouns in the correct order and also makes logical sense.

7. C: The second sentence tells of an unexpected outcome of the first sentence. Choice *A*, Choice *B*, and Choice *D* indicate a logical progression, which does not match this surprise. Only Choice *C* indicates this unexpected twist.

8. B: Choice *A*, Choice *C*, and Choice *D* all relate facts but do not present the kind of general statement that would serve as an effective summary or conclusion. Choice *B* is correct.

9. B: Answer Choice *A* uses the plural form of the verb, when the subject is the pronoun *none*, which needs a singular verb. *C* also uses the wrong verb form and uses the word *all* in place of *none*, which doesn't make sense in the context of the sentence. *D* uses *all* again, and is missing the comma, which is necessary to set the dependent clause off from the independent clause.

10. C: In this answer, the article and subject agree, and the subject and predicate agree. Answer Choice *A* is incorrect because the article *an* and *issues* do not agree in number. *B* is incorrect because an article is needed before *important issue*. D is incorrect because the plural subject *issues* does not agree with the singular verb *is*.

11. D: Choices *A* and *C* use additional words and phrases that aren't necessary. *B* is more concise, but uses the present tense of *is*. This does not agree with the rest of the sentence, which uses past tense. The best choice is *D*, which uses the most concise sentence structure and is grammatically correct.

12. C: Choice *A* is missing the word *that*, which is necessary for the sentence to make sense. Choice *B* pluralizes *trains* and uses the singular form of the word *include*, so it does not agree with the word *set*. Choice *D* changes the verb to *were*, which is in plural form and does not agree with the singular subject.

13. A: Choices *B* and *D* both use the expression *attributed to the fact* incorrectly. It can only be attributed *to* the fact, not *with* or *in* the fact. Choice *C* incorrectly uses a gerund, *saying,* when it should use the present tense of the verb *say*.

14. B: Choice *B* is correct because it uses correct parallel structure of plural nouns. Choice *A* is incorrect because the word *accessory* is in singular form. Choice *C* is incorrect because it pluralizes *makeup*, which is already in plural form. Choice *D* is incorrect because it again uses the singular *accessory*, and it uses the singular *shoe*.

15. D: In a cause/effect relationship, it is correct to begin with the word *because*. This can eliminate both Choices *B* and *C*, which don't clearly show the cause/effect relationship. Choice *A* is incorrect because it uses the past tense, when the main clause is in the present tense. It makes grammatical sense for both parts of the sentence to be in present tense.

16. A: In answer Choice *B*, the present tense form of the verb *consider* creates an independent clause joined to another independent clause with only a comma, which is a comma splice and grammatically incorrect. Choices *C* and *D* use the possessive form of *its*, when it should be the contraction *it's* for *it is*. Choice *D* also includes incorrect comma placement.

17. C: The original sentence states that firefighting is dangerous, making it necessary for firefighters to wear protective gear. The portion of the sentence that needs to be rewritten focuses on the gear, not the dangers, of firefighting. *A*, *B*, and *D* all discuss the danger, not the gear, so *C* is the correct answer.

18. D: The original sentence states that though the sites are popular, they can be dangerous for teens, so *D* is the best choice. Choice *A* does state that there is danger, but it doesn't identify teens and limits it to just one site. Choice *B* repeats the statement from the beginning of the sentence, and *C* says the sites are used too much, which is not the point made in the original sentence.

19. B: The original sentence focuses on how politicians are using the student debt issue to their advantage, so *B* is the best answer choice. Choice *A* says politicians want students' votes, but suggests that it is the reason for student loan debt, which is incorrect. Choice *C* shifts the focus to voters, when the sentence is really about politicians. Choice *D* is vague and doesn't best restate the original meaning of the sentence.

20. A: This answer best matches the meaning of the original sentence, which states that seasoned runners offer advice to new runners because they have complaints of injuries. Choice *B* may be true, but it doesn't mention the complaints of injuries by new runners. Choice *C* may also be true, but it does not match the original meaning of the sentence. Choice *D* does not make sense in the context of the sentence.

Vocabulary

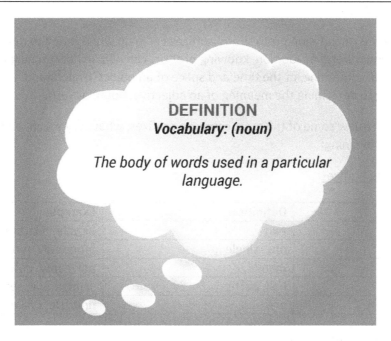

Vocabulary is simply the words a person uses and understands on a daily basis. Having a good vocabulary is important in both written and verbal communications. In law enforcement, officers may have to read court records, police reports, and other legal documents. Many of these materials may contain unfamiliar words, so it's important for officers to learn ways to uncover a word's meaning so they can use it correctly in their own writing.

To understand the challenges of using vocabulary correctly, imagine suddenly being thrust into a foreign country. Not knowing the right words to use when asking for basic necessities (e.g., food, a place to stay, a bathroom) would make everyday life extremely difficult. Asking for help from foreigners who don't share the same vocabulary is hard, since language is what facilitates understanding between people. The more vocabulary words a person understands, the more precisely they can communicate their intentions. This section of the study guide focuses on understanding and deciphering vocabulary through basic grammar.

Prefixes and Suffixes

In the previous section, we went over the particular *spelling* of prefixes and suffixes, and how they changed the root word. In this section, we will look at the *meaning* of various prefixes and suffixes when added to a root word. As mentioned before, a *prefix* is a combination of letters found at the beginning of a word, while a *suffix* is a combination of letters found at the end. A *root word* is the word that comes after the prefix, before the suffix, or between them both. Sometimes a root word can stand on its own without either a prefix or a suffix. More simply put:

Prefix + Root Word = Word

Root Word + Suffix = Word

Prefix + Root Word + Suffix = Word

Root Word = Word

Knowing the definitions of common prefixes and suffixes can help when trying to determine the meaning of an unknown word. In addition, knowing prefixes can help in determining the number of things, the negative of something, or the time and space of an object. Understanding suffix definitions can help when trying to determine the meaning of an adjective, noun, or verb.

The following charts review some of the most common prefixes, what they mean, and how they're used to decipher a word's meaning:

Number and Quantity Prefixes

Prefix	Definition	Example
bi-	two	bicycle, bilateral
mono-	one, single	monopoly, monotone
poly-	many	polygamy, polygon
semi-	half, partly	semiannual, semicircle
uni-	one	unicycle, universal

Here's an example of a number prefix:

The countries signed a *bilateral* agreement; both had to abide by the contract.

Look at the word *bilateral*. If the root word (*lateral*) is unfamiliar, the prefix (*bi-*) can provide a vital clue to its meaning. The prefix *bi-* means *two*, which shows that the agreement involves two of something, most likely the two countries, since *both had to abide by the contract*. This is correct since *bilateral* actually means "involving two parties, usually countries."

Negative Prefixes

Prefix	Definition	Example
a-	without, lack of	amoral, atypical
in-	not, opposing	inability, inverted
non-	not	nonexistent, nonstop
un-	not, reverse	unable, unspoken

Here's an example of a negative prefix:

The patient's *inability* to speak made the doctor wonder what was wrong.

Look at the word *inability.* In the chart above, the prefix *in-* means *not* or *opposing*. By replacing the prefix with *not* and placing it in front of the root word of *ability* (*able*), the meaning of the word becomes clear: *not able*. Therefore, the patient was *not able* to speak.

Time and Space Prefixes

Prefix	Definition	Example
a-	in, on, of, up, to	aloof, associate
ab-	from, away, off	abstract, absent
ad-	to, towards	adept, adjacent
ante-	before, previous	antebellum, antenna
anti-	against, opposing	anticipate, antisocial
cata-	down, away, thoroughly	catacomb, catalogue
circum-	around	circumstance, circumvent
com-	with, together, very	combine, compel
contra-	against, opposing	contraband, contrast
de-	from	decrease, descend
dia-	through, across, apart	diagram, dialect
dis-	away, off, down, not	disregard, disrespect
epi-	upon	epidemic, epiphany
ex-	out	example, exit
hypo-	under, beneath	hypoallergenic, hypothermia
inter-	among, between	intermediate, international
intra-	within	intrapersonal, intravenous
ob-	against, opposing	obtain, obscure
per-	through	permanent, persist
peri-	around	periodontal, periphery
post-	after, following	postdate, postoperative
pre-	before, previous	precede, premeditate
pro-	forward, in place of	program, propel
retro-	back, backward	retroactive, retrofit
sub-	under, beneath	submarine, substantial
super-	above, extra	superior, supersede
trans-	across, beyond, over	transform, transmit
ultra-	beyond, excessively	ultraclean, ultralight

Here's an example of a space prefix:

> The teacher's motivational speech helped *propel* her students toward greater academic achievement.

Look at the word *propel*. The prefix *pro-* means *forward* or *in place of* which indicates something relevant to time and space. *Propel* means to drive or move in a direction (usually forward), so knowing the prefix *pro-* helps interpret that the students are moving forward *toward greater academic achievement*.

Miscellaneous Prefixes

Prefix	Definition	Example
belli-	war, warlike	bellied, belligerent
bene-	well, good	benediction, beneficial
equi-	equal	equidistant, equinox
for-	away, off, from	forbidden, forsaken
fore-	previous	forecast, forebode
homo-	same, equal	homogeneous, homonym
hyper-	excessive, over	hyperextend, hyperactive
in-	in, into	insignificant, invasive
magn-	large	magnetic, magnificent
mal-	bad, poorly, not	maladapted, malnourished
mis-	bad, poorly, not	misplace, misguide
mor-	death	mortal, morgue
neo-	new	neoclassical, neonatal
omni-	all, everywhere	omnipotent, omnipresent
ortho-	right, straight	orthodontist, orthopedic
over-	above	overload, overstock,
pan-	all, entire	panacea, pander
para-	beside, beyond	paradigm, parameter
phil-	love, like	philanthropy, philosophic
prim-	first, early	primal, primer
re-	backward, again	reload, regress
sym-	with, together	symmetry, symbolize
vis-	to see	visual, visibility

Here's another prefix example:

The computer was *primitive*; it still had a floppy disk drive!

The word *primitive* has the prefix *prim-* which indicates being *first* or *early*. *Primitive* means the early stages of evolution or the historical development of something. Therefore, the sentence infers that the computer is an older model because it no longer has a floppy disk drive.

The charts that follow review some of the most common suffixes and include examples of how they're used to determine the meaning of a word. Remember, suffixes are added to the *end* of a root word:

Adjective Suffixes

Suffix	Definition	Example
-able (-ible)	capable of being	teachable, accessible
-esque	in the style of, like	humoresque, statuesque
-ful	filled with, marked by	helpful, deceitful
-ic	having, containing	manic, elastic
-ish	suggesting, like	malnourish, tarnish
-less	lacking, without	worthless, fearless
-ous	marked by, given to	generous, previous

Here's an example of an adjective suffix:

The live model looked so *statuesque* in the window display; she didn't even move!

Look at the word *statuesque*. The suffix *-esque* means *in the style of* or *like*. If something is *statuesque*, it's *in the style of a statue* or *like a statue*. In this sentence, the model looks *like* a statue.

Noun Suffixes

Suffix	Definition	Example
-acy	state, condition	literacy, legacy
-ance	act, condition, fact	distance, importance
-ard	one that does	leotard, billiard
-ation	action, state, result	legislation, condemnation
-dom	state, rank, condition	freedom, kingdom
-er (-or)	office, action	commuter, spectator
-ess	feminine	caress, princess
-hood	state, condition	childhood, livelihood
-ion	action, result, state	communion, position
-ism	act, manner, doctrine	capitalism, patriotism
-ist	worker, follower	stylist, activist
-ity (-ty)	state, quality, condition	community, dirty
-ment	result, action	empowerment, segment
-ness	quality, state	fitness, rudeness
-ship	position	censorship, leadership
-sion (-tion)	state, result	tension, transition
-th	act, state, quality	twentieth, wealth
-tude	quality, state, result	attitude, latitude

Look at the following example of a noun suffix:

The *spectator* cheered when his favorite soccer team scored a goal.

Look at the word *spectator*. The suffix *-or* means *action*. In this sentence, the *action* is to *spectate* (watch something), thus a *spectator* is someone involved in watching something.

Verb Suffixes

Suffix	Definition	Example
-ate	having, showing	facilitate, integrate
-en	cause to be, become	frozen, written
-fy	make, cause to have	modify, rectify
-ize	cause to be, treat with	realize, sanitize

Here's an example of a verb suffix:

The preschool had to *sanitize* the toys every Tuesday and Thursday.

In the word *sanitize*, the suffix *-ize* means *cause to be* or *treat with*. By adding the suffix *-ize* to the root word *sanitary*, the meaning of the word becomes active: *cause to be sanitary*.

Context Clues

It's common to encounter unfamiliar words in written communication. When faced with an unknown word, there are certain "tricks" that can be used to uncover its meaning. *Context clues* are words or phrases within a sentence or paragraph that provide hints about a word and its definition. For example, if an unfamiliar word is anchored to a noun with other attached words as clues, these can help decipher the word's meaning. Consider the following example:

After the treatment, Grandma's natural rosy cheeks looked *wan* and ghostlike.

The unfamiliar word is *wan.* The first clue to its meaning is in the phrase *After the treatment,* which implies that something happened after a procedure (possibly medical). A second clue is the word *rosy,* which describes Grandma's natural cheek color that changed after the treatment. Finally, the word *ghostlike* infers that Grandma's cheeks now look white. By using the context clues in the sentence, the meaning of the word *wan* (which means *pale*) can be deciphered.

Below are some additional ways to use context clues to uncover the meaning of an unknown word:

Contrasts
Look for context clues that *contrast* the unknown word. When reading a sentence with an unfamiliar word, look for a contrasting or opposing word or idea. Here's an example:

Since Mary didn't cite her research sources, she lost significant points for *plagiarizing* the content of her report.

In this sentence, *plagiarizing* is the unfamiliar word. Notice that when Mary *didn't cite her research sources,* it resulted in her losing points for *plagiarizing the content of her report*. These contrasting ideas infer that Mary did something wrong with the content. This makes sense because the definition of *plagiarizing* is "taking the work of someone else and passing it off as your own."

Contrasts often use words like *but, however, although,* or phrases like *on the other hand.* For example:

The *gargantuan* television won't fit in my car, but it will cover the entire wall in the den.

The unfamiliar word is *gargantuan*. Notice that the television is too big to fit in a car, <u>but</u> *it will cover the entire wall in the den*. This infers that the television is extremely large, which is correct, since the word *gargantuan* means "enormous."

Synonyms

Another method is to brainstorm possible synonyms for the unknown word. *Synonyms* are words with the same or similar meanings (e.g., *strong* and *sturdy*). To do this, substitute synonyms one at a time, reading the sentence after each to see if the meaning is clear. By replacing an unknown word with a known one, it may be possible to uncover its meaning. For example:

Gary's clothes were *saturated* after he fell into the swimming pool.

In this sentence, the word *saturated* is unknown. To brainstorm synonyms for *saturated*, think about what happens to Gary's clothes after falling into the swimming pool. They'd be *soaked* or *wet*, both of which turn out to be good synonyms to try since the actual meaning of *saturated* is "thoroughly soaked."

Antonyms

Sometimes sentences contain words or phrases that oppose each other. Opposite words are known as *antonyms* (e.g., *hot* and *cold*). For example:

Although Mark seemed *tranquil*, you could tell he was actually nervous as he paced up and down the hall.

The unknown word here is *tranquil*. The sentence says that Mark was in fact not *tranquil* but was instead *actually nervous*. The opposite of the word *nervous* is *calm*, which is the meaning of the word *tranquil*.

Explanations or Descriptions

Explanations or *descriptions* of other things in the sentence can also provide clues to an unfamiliar word. Take the following example:

Golden Retrievers, Great Danes, and Pugs are the top three *breeds* competing in the dog show.

If the word *breeds* is unknown, look at the sentence for an explanation or description that provides a clue. The subjects (*Golden Retrievers*, *Great Danes*, and *Pugs*) describe different types of dogs. This description helps uncover the meaning of the word *breeds* which is "a particular type or group of animals."

Inferences

Sometimes there are clues to an unknown word that infer or suggest its meaning. These *inferences* can be found either within the sentence where the word appears or in a sentence that precedes or follows it. Look at the following example:

The *wretched* old lady was kicked out of the restaurant. She was so mean and nasty to the waiter!

Here the word *wretched* is unknown. The first sentence states that the *old lady was kicked out of the restaurant*, but it doesn't say why. The sentence that follows tells us why: *She was so mean and nasty to the waiter!* This infers that the old lady was *kicked out* because she was *so mean and nasty* or, in other words, *wretched*.

When preparing for a vocabulary test, try reading challenging materials to learn new words. If a word on the test is unfamiliar, look for prefixes and suffixes to help uncover what the word means and eliminate incorrect answers. If two answers both seem right, determine if there are any differences between them and then select the word that best fits. Context clues in the sentence or paragraph can also help to uncover the meaning of an unknown word. By learning new vocabulary words, a person can expand their knowledge base and improve the quality and effectiveness of their written communications.

Practice Questions

Directions: Read each sentence carefully and select the answer that is closest in meaning to the <u>underlined </u>*word. Use prefix/suffix definitions and context clues to help eliminate incorrect answers.*

1. Only one of the thieves who robbed the jewelry store was caught since his <u>accomplice</u> got away.
    a. Roommate
    b. Brother
    c. Partner
    d. Manager

2. The congressman denied the <u>allegation</u> that he'd voted in favor of the bill in exchange for a campaign donation.
    a. Claim
    b. Reptile
    c. Highway
    d. Interrogation

3. During the <u>arraignment</u> in front of the judge, Tommy pleaded not guilty to driving under the influence of alcohol.
    a. Wedding
    b. Proceeding
    c. Bouquet
    d. Conclusion

4. The violent offender was convicted of <u>battery</u> for using a baseball bat to strike his victim.
    a. Voltage
    b. Assault
    c. Flattery
    d. Arson

5. The gang members in Shelly's neighborhood tried to <u>coerce</u> her into selling drugs, but she refused to be bullied.
    a. Pay
    b. Discourage
    c. Gender
    d. Pressure

6. The company treasurer was found guilty of <u>embezzling</u> $50,000 from the company's bank account to pay for the remodeling of his home.
    a. Bedazzling
    b. Stealing
    c. Decorating
    d. Borrowing

7. The judge <u>exonerated</u> Susan of all charges, so she left the courtroom a free woman.
    a. Cleared
    b. Executed
    c. Tried
    d. Convicted

8. When officers arrived on the scene of the deadly crash, they learned there had been one <u>fatality</u>.
    a. Birth
    b. Attraction
    c. Death
    d. Celebration

9. The unsuspecting art collector didn't realize the painting was a <u>forgery</u> until after it was appraised, so she became the 13th victim of the con artist.
    a. Antique
    b. Operation
    c. Sculpture
    d. Fake

10. The criminals wore gloves so they wouldn't leave behind any <u>latent</u> fingerprints.
    a. Hidden
    b. Painted
    c. Vinyl
    d. Visible

11. The state declared a <u>moratorium</u> on executions after new evidence cleared one death row inmate of his crime.
    a. Funeral
    b. Postponement
    c. Speech
    d. Hospitalization

12. The witness said the <u>perpetrator</u> wore a black ski mask and a blonde wig during the home invasion.
    a. Model
    b. Student
    c. Criminal
    d. Dancer

13. Though Miss Johnson swore to tell the truth under oath, she actually tried to <u>prevaricate</u> and claimed she didn't remember any details.
    a. Steal
    b. Impregnate
    c. Lie
    d. Confess

14. The city's first responders must follow <u>protocol</u> when handling calls for cases of domestic violence.
    a. Guidelines
    b. Internist
    c. Requests
    d. Evidence

15. After the riot broke out, officers had to use strong measures to <u>quell</u> the angry crowd.
    a. Wave
    b. Count
    c. Incite
    d. Calm

Answer Explanations

1. C: *Partner*: a person who takes part in a plan with another or other persons

Accomplice: a person who joins another person in the act of carrying out a plan (most likely an illegal or unethical one)

2. A: *Claim*: a declaration that something is the truth without the accompaniment of evidence

Allegation: a claim or assertion of some wrongdoing, typically made without proof

3. B: *Proceeding*: the steps of carrying out the law within an institution

Arraignment: the courtroom proceeding where a defendant is apprised of the charges against them and enters a plea of guilty or not guilty

4. B: *Assault*: to attack suddenly and unlawfully

Battery: an assault where the assailant makes physical contact with another person

5. D: *Pressure*: to influence someone to do a particular thing

Coerce: to persuade an unwilling person to do something by using pressure, intimidation, or threats

6. B: *Stealing*: the act of taking a thing from somebody that isn't one's own

Embezzling: to defraud someone or to steal property (often money) entrusted into one's care

7. A: *Cleared*: to be absolved of misunderstanding or doubt

Exonerated: to be pronounced not guilty of criminal charges

8. C: *Death*: the event of a person's life ending

Fatality: a death that occurs as the result of an accident, disaster, war, or disease

9. D: *Fake*: an imitation of reality; a simulation

Forgery: to create or imitate something (e.g., an object or document) with the intent to deceive others or profit from the sale of it

10. A: *Hidden*: something kept out of sight or concealed

Latent: a thing that's hidden, or something that exists but hasn't been developed yet

11. B: *Postponement*: to hold off on a scheduled activity until a later date

Moratorium: a legal postponement or waiting period set by some authority to suspend activity

12. C: *Criminal*: someone who is guilty of a crime

Perpetrator: the person who commits a crime

13. C: *Lie*: to state a contradiction of the truth; to deceive

Prevaricate: to deliberately evade the truth or lie in order to mislead

14. A: *Guidelines*: a set of standards created for a future action

Protocol: official guidelines or procedures that must be followed

15. D: *Calm*: to make tranquil or serene

Quell: to calm, quiet, or put an end to something

Reasoning

Law enforcement officers use their powers of observation to gather information. Through their reasoning skill-sets, they'll make inferences and draw conclusions about information and evidence.

Very broadly, reasoning is an approach to thinking that prioritizes logic. Law enforcement officers use reasoning every day when forming judgments about suspects, piecing together timelines, and evaluating crime scenes.

There are three general types of reasoning problems:

- Comparative Values
- Numerical Series
- Similar Words

These items on the exam require searches for patterns, similarities, and relationships in order to choose the correct answer. There will be lists of statements, numbers, or words, and test takers will analyze the given information in order to answer the question.

Comparative Values

A *comparative value* item provides details about specific subjects, like types of fruit or family members, and then asks that comparisons be drawn between them. There are two possible tasks:

- Order the subjects from *least to greatest* or *greatest to least*
- Find *the value* of a certain subject

When encountering a comparative value item, it's helpful to make a list and fill it in according to information given in the prompt. Everything needed to answer this type of question correctly is in the question. Here's an example:

> A vehicle rental company stocks cars, vans, busses, and trucks. The company ranks their vehicles by popularity so that they know what to buy when expanding their business. Cars are ranked between vans and trucks. Trucks are more popular than vans. Buses are ranked lowest. Which type of vehicle is rented the most?
>
> a. Cars
> b. Vans
> c. Busses
> d. Trucks

C   V   T   B

The items being compared are the prompt's subjects. In this question, there are cars, vans, buses, and trucks. Assigning them a letter or an image, as illustrated above, is a helpful way to list them quickly. For this question, the first letter of each vehicle represents the subject: C (car), V (van), T (truck), and B (bus).

Note what the prompt actually asks. In this prompt, the goal is to find which vehicle is rented *the most*. Thus the list needs to be ordered from *most to least*:

Vehicles Rented – Most to Least

Determine which information is stated outright, meaning it is known for sure. In this prompt, *buses are ranked the lowest,* so buses can be placed at the bottom of the list:

Vehicles Rented – Most to Least
B

Next, look through the prompt for more information. This prompt states that *cars are ranked between vans and trucks*, so the list can look one of two ways:

Vehicles Rented – Most to Least Possibility 1	Vehicles Rented – Most to Least Possibility 2
V	T
C	C
T	V
B	B

To decide which list is correct, look for the last piece of information given in the prompt. In this prompt, *trucks are more popular than vans.* Which one of the lists shows that to be true?

Vehicles Rented – Most to Least
T
C
V
B

Revisit the final question to determine the response. *Which vehicle is being rented the most?* The answer is *D*, Trucks.

Numerical Series

A *numerical series* item presents a list of numbers and asks test takers to determine what the next number should be. The key to answering this type of question correctly is to understand *the relationship between the numbers* in the series. Do they increase or decrease, and at what rate? Is there a pattern? Here's an example:

> Identify the next number in the series: 7, 14, 21, 28, 35, …
> a. 42
> b. 28
> c. 47
> d. 50

First, decide if the numbers in the list are *increasing* or *decreasing*. Generally, if numbers increase, it is indicative of addition or multiplication. If they decrease, subtraction or division is more likely.

The numbers in this list are *increasing*: 7, 14, 21, 28, 35.

Here's a strategy to determine *the rate* at which they are increasing:

7, 14, 21, 28, 35

+7   +7   +7   +7

The numbers in the list are increasing by 7. The rate of increase is constant throughout the list. Note that not all lists will increase or decrease at a constant rate.

To find the answer to this question, simply continue the rate of increase by adding 7 to 35. The answer is *A*, 42.

Here's a more complicated example:

> Identify the next number in the series: 2, 3, 5, 9, 17…
> a. 24
> b. 33
> c. 37
> d. 39

Again, the first thing to do is decide if the numbers in the list are increasing or decreasing. The numbers in this list are *increasing*: 2, 3, 5, 9, 17.

Next, figure out the rate of increase:

2,   3,   5,   9,   17

+1   +2   +4   +8

Notice that, in this question, the rate of increase is not constant. The question needs to be solved by looking for a pattern in the rate of increase.

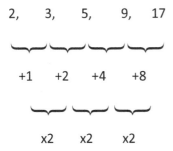

1, 2, 4, and 8 are all *multiples of 2*: 1 x 2 = 2, 2 x 2 = 4, 4 x 2 = 8. What is needed to continue this pattern? *8 x 2.*

Given that 8 x 2 = 16, 16 is the next number in the rate of increase.

2,   3,   5,   9,   17

+1   +2   +4   +8   +16

x2   x2   x2   x2

So, 16 must be added to the last number in the list to find the answer: 17 + 16 = 33. The answer is *B*, 33.

Similar Words

In *similar words* questions, there will be a set of four words. Three of the words will be similar, and one will be different. The goal is to choose the one word that is *unlike* the other three.

The key to answering these questions correctly is to e*stablish the relationship between the three similar words.* The word that does not share that relationship with the others will be the answer. Here's an example:

> Three of the following words are similar, while one is different. Select the word that is different.
>   a. Pants
>   b. Closet
>   c. Dresses
>   d. Skirts

First, consider what the *theme* of the words is. The theme of this list seems to be *clothing.* Next, start with choice *A* and consider how this word relates to choice *B*. Pants can *be kept* in a closet.

In choices *C* and *D*, dresses and skirts, like pants, can also be kept in a closet. So, three out of four of the words are articles of clothing that can be kept in a closet, rendering *closet* the word that is unlike the others. The answer is *B*, Closet.

Here's another example:

Three of the following words are similar, while one is different. Select the word that is different.

   a. Book
   b. Magazine
   c. Newspaper
   d. Reading

In this question, the theme is *reading*, which is also one of the answer choices. Choices *A*, *B*, and *C* are things that can be read. Though choice *D*, reading, does relate to the other answer choices, it does not relate in the same way. Reading is a verb, not an object that can be read, so the word that does not belong is D, Reading.

Practice Questions

Directions: Officers often face situations in which they need to determine how different pieces of information relate to one another. In this section, you will be presented with information, such as a group or ordered series of facts, numbers, letters, or words. Your task is to study the various pieces of information and try to understand how they relate to one another. Mark the letter that identifies your choice on your answer sheet.

1. Three of the following words are similar, while one is different. Which one is different?
   a. Student
   b. Teacher
   c. Desk
   d. Principal

2. The families who live on Gardenia Drive keep dogs, cats, and rabbits as pets. There are 3 more cats than dogs. There are 5 more dogs than rabbits. There are 2 rabbits. How many cats live on Gardenia Drive?
   a. 10
   b. 4
   c. 2
   d. 11

3. Which of the following is the next number in the series: 2, 13, 4, 14, 8, 15…?
   a. 16
   b. 17
   c. 32
   d. 14

4. A local librarian conducts a poll to gauge what types of baked goods should be sold at the library fundraiser. Cookies are ranked between cakes and pies. Pies are ranked higher than cakes. Cream puffs receive the least number of votes. Which type of baked goods receives the most votes?
   a. Cookies
   b. Cakes
   c. Pies
   d. Cream puffs

5. Three of the following words are similar, while one is different. Which one is different?
   a. Roof
   b. Skylight
   c. Ceiling
   d. Floor

6. Which of the following is the next number in the series: 84, 80, 76, 72, 68…?
   a. 75
   b. 67
   c. 64
   d. 70

7. Which of the following is the next number in the series: 17, 18, 20, 23, 27…?
    a. 29
    b. 33
    c. 23
    d. 32

8. After school, Andrew, Matt and Geeta spend time watching television. Andrew watches more television than Geeta, but less than Matt. Which of the following lists from most to least the friends in order of how much television they watch after school?
    a. Andrew, Matt, Geeta
    b. Not enough information
    c. Geeta, Andrew, Matt
    d. Matt, Andrew, Geeta

9. Three of the following words are similar, while one is different. Which one is different?
    a. Notebook
    b. Pencil
    c. Pen
    d. Crayon

10. Which of the following is the next number in the series: 41, 30, 42, 29, 43, 28…?
    a. 30
    b. 44
    c. 43
    d. 41

11. Alejandro, Jennifer and Walt are competing in their track team's 500-meter dash. Jennifer finished behind Walt but ahead of Alejandro. Who won the race?
    a. Alejandro
    b. Jennifer
    c. Walt
    d. Not enough information

12. Which of the following is the next number in the series: 144, 133, 130, 119, 116…?
    a. 113
    b. 105
    c. 127
    d. 98

13. Three of the following words are similar, while one is different. Which one is different?
    a. Lake
    b. Ocean
    c. River
    d. Boat

14. Which of the following is the next number in the series: 288, 144, 72, 36, 18…?
    a. 4
    b. 12
    c. 6
    d. 9

15. On their driving test, Anna earned 97 points, 12 points more than Michael. Michael scored 10 points higher than Tom, who scored 6 points lower than Jaime. What was Tom's score?
    a. 109
    b. 22
    c. 75
    d. 91

16. Which of the following is the next number in the series: 3, 9, 27, 81, 243…?
    a. 486
    b. 729
    c. 121
    d. 356

Answer Explanations

1. C: The word *desk* is not like the other three. A student, teacher, and principal are all people who are found in a school setting. A desk is an inanimate object that can be found in a school setting, rendering it different from the other three words.

2. A: The correct answer is 10. According to the prompt, there are 2 rabbits on Gardenia Drive. If there are 5 more dogs than rabbits, then there are 7 dogs. If there are 3 more cats than dogs, then 10 cats live on Gardenia Drive.

3. A: The next number in the series is 16. In this series, two patterns of increase can be found. Every other number either doubles or increases by one. So, to find the next number in the series, decide which pattern the missing number should continue. Because 2x2 is 4 and 4x2 is 8, the missing number is 16.

4. C: The correct answer is pies. According to the prompt, cookies are ranked between cakes and pies, and pies are ranked higher than cakes. At this point, the list should read *pies, cookies,* and *cakes.* The last information in the prompt is that cream puffs received the least number of votes, so *pies* remains at the top of the list, having the most votes received.

5. D: The word *floor* is not like the other three. A roof, skylight, and ceiling are all elements of a house or building positioned *above*. The floor is positioned *below*, making it unlike the other three words.

6. C: The next number in the series is 64. In this series, each successive number is 4 less than the number that preceded it. So, to find the next number in the series, subtract 4 from the previous number.

7. D: The next number in the series is 32. In this series, the numbers increase by *one more with each successive number*. So, there is an increase of 1 between the first two numbers, an increase of 2 between the second and third numbers, an increase of 3 between the third and fourth numbers, and an increase of 4 between the fourth and fifth numbers. The next number in the series should be 5 more than the last number given.

8. D: The correct answer is Matt, Andrew, Geeta. According to the prompt, Andrew watches more television than Geeta. Since the goal is to rank the friends in order of how much television they watch *from most to least*, the list should read the following way so far: Andrew, Geeta. The prompt goes on to say that Andrew watches less television than Matt, so Matt must be added to the list above Andrew.

9. A: The word *notebook* is not like the other three. A pencil, pen, and crayon can all be used to write or draw. A notebook is something that is written or drawn *in*, rendering it different from the other three words.

10. B: The next number in the series is 44. Beginning with the first number in the series, every other number *increases by 1*. Beginning with the second number, every other number *decreases by 1*. So, to find the next number in the series, decide which pattern the missing number should continue. The missing number should continue the pattern of increasing by 1 starting with the first number in the series. Looking only at that pattern, the series reads 41...42...43. Continuing that pattern, the missing number should be 44.

11. D: Out of the three on this particular team, Walt came in first. However, it's unclear whether or not other teams were participating in this race. Thus, there is insufficient information to determine whether or not Walt won the race.

12. B: The next number in the series is 105. In this series, the numbers are decreasing. The gap between each number is either 11 or 3. Following this pattern, the next number should be 11 less than the last number.

13. D: The word *boat* is not like the other three. A lake, ocean, and river are all bodies of water. A boat is a vessel used to traverse bodies of water, rendering it different from the other three words.

14. D: The next number in the series is 9. In this series, each successive number decreases by half.

15. C: Tom's score was 75. According to the prompt, Anna earned 97 points, which was 12 more than Michael. Michael earned 85 points, which is 10 more than Tom.

16. B: The next number in the series is 729. In this series, each number

Memory

The Memory section of the Corrections Exam assesses a candidate's observational skills and his or her ability to recall facts and information. This is a very important skill that corrections officers must employ daily during routine job duties. For example, they are regularly required to observe prison inmates and gather information pertaining to the behavior they witnessed that they must recall at a later point in time.

On the exam, this section is typically composed of a couple of drawings or photographs that are followed by a series of multiple-choice questions. The questions are not viewable until the image is removed. Test takers examine each graphic one at a time, for approximately one to five minutes (depending on the state administering the test as well as the complexity of the image) and then the image is removed. During the observation period, it is recommended that test takers study the image as carefully as possible, first examining the overall scene and then studying it more closely to identify and memorize details. The questions that follow pertain to details from the graphic and must be completed from memory. Access to review the image again is not permitted. Because the questions pertaining to the image may address the picture on a general level as well as specific details, both elements need to be examined. For example, test takers may encounter an image of a prison cell containing several inmates who are fighting. One question may address the image as a whole, such as: "*what is the general mood of the image?*" Answer choices may be options such as *triumphant, hopeful, agitated*, and *peaceful.* In this case, *agitated* is the best choice. The majority of the questions will be about more specific details from the image. For example, questions for this same image may ask how many inmates were present in the scene, what time was displayed on the wall clock, what was the position of the cell door, or how many bars were running vertically on the window.

There are a variety of strategies that candidates employ to improve their scores in this section. Most test takers start by examining the entire image for a few seconds and then moving from this broad view to an increasingly specific study. Some people find that it works best to examine the picture in quadrants or in designated sections individually in a predetermined order to ensure that the entire image is studied without leaving gaps. Other candidates employ a variety of strategies depending on the particular image. For example, they may study the people first and then the environment surrounding the scene for an outdoor picture or start by looking at the walls and then the middle of the room indoors. Other test takers start by trying to identify context clues from the scene, such as the sun position or weather in outdoor scenes or the clock time indoors to determine the season or time of day. Then, they may move on to try to count specific figures or subjects in the scene and identify distinguishing characteristics between such figures. For example, are there a different number of males and females present? Is someone wearing a distinguishing piece of clothing such as a hat? Exam questions often address things such as the time, place, and setting of the graphic. Others ask test takers to recall the number of certain items present, or to answer questions about a specific item in the image, which can be better answered if distinguishing features of the items are noted during the study period.

It is recommended that test takers practice with a variety of images and strategies to familiarize themselves with the process and to identify those methods that work best. A sample graphic similar to those that may be encountered on the exam is provided below. Test takers should study the graphic for two minutes and then completely remove it from their view while attempting the practice questions. Test takers can practice this section an unlimited number of times with the help of a partner or friend.

The partner can find any type of image and generate a few questions about it and then pass it to the test candidate to attempt.

Practice Image

Directions:

Examine the image below for two minutes then remove it from view. Answer the questions that follow the image without referring back to the image. Do not read the questions during the image review period.

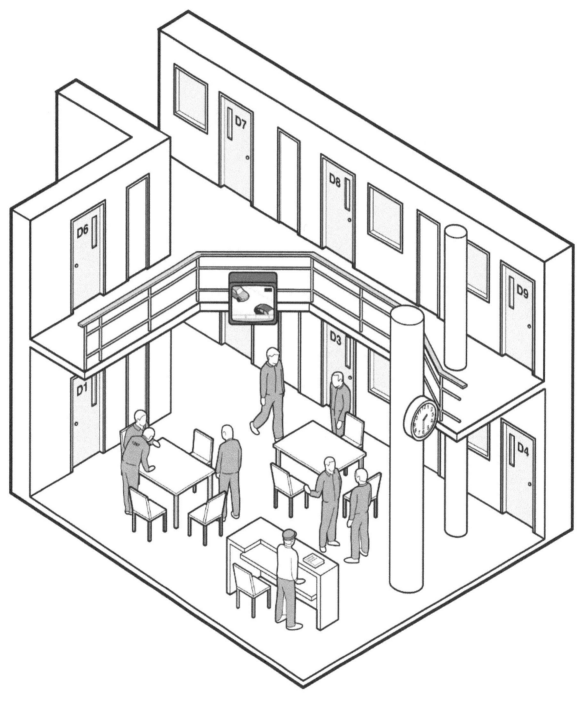

1. How many doors are located on the second floor?
   a. 1
   b. 2
   c. 3
   d. 4

2. How many inmates are located at the table on the left?
   a. 3
   b. 4
   c. 5
   d. 6

3. What time is it?
   a. 7:50
   b. 2:30
   c. 12:10
   d. 4:00

4. What is written on the right most door downstairs?
   a. D4
   b. D9
   c. C9
   d. C4

5. What was on the television?
   a. Animals
   b. A cartoon
   c. Cars
   d. The news

Answers

1. D
2. A
3. B
4. A
5. C

Understanding and Applying Correctional Directives, Procedures, and Regulations

Corrections

The term *correctional* or *corrections* refers to the detention and/or supervision of an individual either charged with or convicted of a crime. This detention may be either court ordered or as a condition of confinement and subsequent release by a correction department. If the individual has been charged, but not yet convicted, then they are generally sentenced to either jail, pending the disposition of their case; probation; or released, pending their next hearing. If the individual has been sentenced, then they will likely be in a prison. Jails and prisons have distinct differences, in that jails are generally for pending court cases and short-term sentences, while prisons are reserved for convicted offenders with longer sentences.

Individuals on some type of monitoring in a community setting such as probation, parole, electronic monitoring, or assigned to a halfway house, day reporting center, work release, or any other community-based program, are considered to be in a *community corrections* setting.

The Bureau of Justice Statistics estimates there are over two million individuals currently incarcerated in the United States, with another six million on some type of community-based supervision, known as community corrections.

Criminal Justice System

The criminal justice system consists of three main functions: law enforcement, the judicial process, and corrections. The courts are the main part of the judicial process that determines the need for punishment. Courts operate on federal, state, and local levels. Those individuals sentenced on a federal level end up in the custody or supervision of the United States Federal Bureau of Prisons. Individuals sentenced on the state level populate the state facilities. Offenders who violate local laws may serve sentences of one year or less in county facilities; otherwise, they will be sent to state facilities for longer sentences.

Standards

Before the 1970's, jails and prisons traditionally operated with little or no oversight, which resulted in poor confinement conditions. As an outcome of riots triggered by these poor conditions, several oversight agencies emerged and legislative changes resulted in vastly improved minimum standards of inmate care. One of the first oversight agencies was the American Correctional Association (ACA) – a non-profit organization that developed a system of standards and audits to monitor quality and performance at correctional institutions.

Also emerging as a result of the prison riots of the 1970's, the National Institute of Corrections (NIC) was formed in 1974, as a training and audit mechanism of the Federal Bureau of Prisons. The goal of the NIC was to improve conditions and training at federal, state, and local facilities.

More recently in 2003, federal legislation created the Prison Rape Elimination Act (PREA), which is federal law that guides the reporting and monitoring of sexual assault in all United States jails or prisons.

In addition to federal oversight, many state and local correction agencies are under court degrees or mandates as a result of litigation, to ensure minimum standards of care for inmate medical treatment, inmate visiting, access to law libraries, and religious practice, among other conditions of confinement.

Facility Accreditation

Although not mandated in all facilities, many correctional facilities seek American Correctional Association (ACA) accreditation. The accreditation is a rigorous process, wherein the facility, in preparation for an audit, must meet universal standards set by the association. The standards cover a range of multiple disciplines, including categories such as environmental health, safety, and security. Scores are awarded for each criterion identified. Facilities must maintain the level or standards of the ACA or they risk losing accreditation. Accreditation can be expensive, and the cost of the accreditation is borne by the facility; however, the outcome generally provides a safer and more secure environment for inmates and custodial staff.

National Commission on Correctional Health Care (NCCHC)

Much like the American Correctional Association (ACA), the National Commission on Correctional Healthcare (NCCHC) is a nonprofit organization with a mission to standardize the best practices for inmate healthcare. The NCCHC offers guidance and support to the healthcare programs of prisons and jails, while offering a certification program for correctional healthcare professionals.

Audits

Independent and self-audits are a tool to ensure correctional facilities are meeting, and exceeding, established correctional standards. In general, to meet the criteria for American Correctional Association compliance, the facility is given an audit document upon which they will be tested at a later time. The auditor will come in at a scheduled time and grade the facility on the criteria discussed. Failing an audit can lead to employee discipline and loss of funding.

Male Inmate Population

The United States incarcerates by far more inmates per capita than any other country in the world, with over two million people presently incarcerated and another six million in community corrections. Of the incarcerated population, the majority are male prisoners, who represent approximately 93% of the incarcerated population in the United States. Over the course of the last three decades, the incarceration rate has risen in the United States, but with recent changes to sentencing guidelines and other prison reform activities, this trend is starting to reverse.

The ethnic makeup of prison populations tends to vary, based upon the geographic area served or the mission of the agency that directs the custody. For example, because illegal immigration is a federal violation, a large subset of the population of the Federal Bureau of Prisons is made up of Hispanic inmates with detention issues associated with immigration. Because the Federal government prosecutes more white collar crimes than other agencies, its white male population is greater than is generally found in local jails in New York City or Los Angeles – cities that typically prosecute a greater number of lower level drug offenses in minority neighborhoods. It should be noted that despite the high incarceration rate in the United States, approximately 95% of all prisoners will one day be released to the community.

Female Inmate Population

The current female incarceration rate is estimated to be between 6-8% of the total overall incarcerated population. The majority of female offenders are minorities who are serving time for non-violent crimes related to drug-related offenses stemming from drug dependency. Female prisoners generally require more medical and mental health services than do their male counterparts. Some correctional facilities also have nurseries to enable pregnant prisoners to keep their babies with them for a short time after birth, provided they meet established program criteria.

Juvenile Justice Corrections Program

To be classified as a juvenile or adolescent prisoner, individuals must fall within established age ranges in their jurisdiction – typically between 12 to 21 years of age. According to the Office of Juvenile Justice and Delinquency Programs (OJJDP), there are approximately 50,000 juveniles currently under correctional supervision, in what OJJDP classifies as residential housing. The juvenile inmates are predominantly minorities who are charged with crimes against persons and property.

The juvenile population is difficult to manage both because of the need to supply additional programs and services such as state-mandated school programs, and because criminal propensity tends to peak in the 16-18 years of age range. As prisoners age, their criminal behavior tends to decline.

Problems in Prison Populations

There are a multitude of problems faced by prison administrators. The following are some of the significant problems correctional administrators face:

- Drug use: Many prisoners have a history of drug use and require extensive treatment programs to help stabilize their addiction and prevent the use of illegal contraband drugs while incarcerated.

- Medical issues: Because most new prisoners have not maintained adequate healthcare outside of prison, they arrive as new admission prisoners with a host of medical issues, possibly including communicable diseases.

- Mental health issues: At any given time, more than half of a correctional population may be receiving mental health treatment. Specialized treatment plans, enhanced observation, and special housing are required to reduce self-harm and aggressive behavior.

- Security-related issues: Gangs are prevalent in inmate populations and a classification system to separate prisoners based upon gender, age, security level, and a host of other factors must be considered to foster a safe environment.

These are just a few examples of the many challenges correctional administrators face in providing a safe and secure correctional environment.

Federal Prison System

The Federal Bureau of Prisons (BOP) was founded in 1930 in response to a growing number of people convicted of federal crimes. Today, the BOP houses approximately 200,000 prisoners and employs approximately 40,000 staff members. They manage over 122 facilities throughout the United States and list public safety, national security, and inmate programming among their highest goals. The federal inmate population consists of approximately one-third Hispanics, one-third African Americans, and one-third Caucasians, with a small percentage of Asians, American Indians, and others representing the remaining fractional shares. Drug-related offenses make up the majority of incarcerations in the federal system. Over 93% of the current population within the Federal Bureau of Prisons is male.

Because of overcrowding issues in the past, the Federal Bureau of Prisons has sought to outsource some of its inmate population to non-governmental companies that house prisoners for a profit. Presently, there are approximately 20,000 federal prisoners being held in privately-owned, for-profit facilities.

Private Corrections Industry

Prison populations grew tremendously in the 1970's and 1980's, fueled by strict sentencing guidelines and harsh drug laws, in an effort to curb epidemic drug use. As governments began to run out of room to house the growing inmate population, private industry answered the call. In 1983, a private company called the Corrections Corporation of America (CCA) opened their first facility to accept inmates for a profit.

Companies such as CCA and the GEO Group, which are both publicly traded, began to provide beds for incarcerated inmates as a solution to overcrowding. Many of these vendors have expanded their services to include medical and mental health services and residential programs for re-entry, which help offenders prepare to re-enter the community.

The Auburn and Pennsylvania Correctional Systems

Early correctional philosophy was modeled after the *Pennsylvania system*, which took root in the Quaker religion within the state of Pennsylvania. The Pennsylvania system placed a heavy emphasis on solitary confinement, which the Quakers felt would lead to penitence and reform. Critics of the Pennsylvania system felt it caused more harm than good and it was replaced by the *Auburn system*, which was named after a correctional facility operated in New York State in the 1800's. The Auburn system permitted work and communal activity with other prisoners during the day and resorted to stark silence and containment in single bed cells in the evening.

Boot Camps

The 1980's saw an emphasis on prison boot camps, in which the prisoner would elect to participate in a program with strict mandatory programs infused with physical exercise, modeling a military style of operation. Inmates could even receive a reduced sentence in exchange for agreeing to participate in the program.

While some inmate boot camps are still in operation today, evidence-based research suggests these programs do not significantly reduce recidivism and, in some cases, they can foster increased aggression in inmates and deliver a poorer outcome.

Direct Supervision

There are several methods of supervision within a correctional setting. The methods of supervision in a particular area may depend upon the classification or security level of the prisoner. For example, some prisoners under mental health evaluation may require a ratio of one officer to one inmate to prevent suicide. In dormitory settings, there may be one officer to 50 or more inmates, if they are considered low risk prisoners. In other supervision situations, there might not be an officer in the living area and instead, supervision is maintained through camera surveillance and electronic gates. It is considered direct supervision when an officer is actively assigned to patrol the inmates' living quarters.

Unit Management Approach

Unit management is a system of supervision where the correctional facility is divided into mini units. Each unit has a unit manager and unit team members who carry out a specialized and directed mission within their unit. They still follow all the rules and policies of the institution, but steady unit team members can gain experience with the population within their unit. This permits unit consistency and stability, which leads to a safer environment.

Communicating Policies to Inmates

There are several ways to disseminate information regarding the facility's policy rules and regulations to the inmates. Some of those methods include:

- The new admission process: As part of the new admission process, each incoming inmate receives a copy of the facility's rules and regulations.

- Orientation: Inmates usually attend an orientation shortly after arriving at the facility, where the rules, programs, and services are explained.

- Signage: Correctional facilities generally have a great deal of signage to alert and remind inmates of the rules and procedures.

- Counseling: Inmates are usually assigned to a counselor, who helps guide them through the facility process.

- Law Library: Inmates have access to a law library where they can access and research the facility's rules and policies.

- Housing units/service areas: Inmates can informally ask facility staff in their housing unit or at a service area questions regarding policies.

Emergency Plans

Correctional facilities can experience a wide variety of emergencies including, but not limited to, slashings, stabbings, deaths, riots, and escapes. It is for this reason that the correctional facility has specific emergency plans maintained in their control room. Upon notification of a specific emergency, the shift commander can easily access the plans and direct the emergency response step-by-step, according to that plan.

The emergency plan identifies who gets notified and what response actions the shift commander must take to control or contain the situation.

Civil Disturbances

Because correctional facilities get exposure to the public and media through inmate visits, media response to facility emergencies, and possibly protestors, correctional facilities must have a plan to protect their perimeter from civil disturbances, which might otherwise affect normal facility operations.

The plan should include inter-agency response information if police, fire, or other agencies are needed for the emergency. A clear lane for emergency response vehicles to arrive and depart the facility should always be maintained. To avoid affecting normal facility functions, the plan should also provide a staging area for media to be contained and consider using an offsite command post. The civil response plan should also consider maintaining a secure perimeter for the facility to prevent escapes, the introduction of contraband, or fires.

Work or Food Strikes

Food strikes are not uncommon in correctional facilities. To get the attention of the correctional administration, media, or both, inmates may resort to the passive resistance of a food strike. Therefore, correctional facilities maintain a food strike emergency plan. This plan sets thresholds for the number of meals skipped by the inmates or the number of inmates participating in a mass food strike before a response is triggered. Settlement usually involves discussion with the inmates or with the most influential inmate. Inmates should be encouraged to remain peaceful and to utilize the formal communication mechanisms already established in the facility. Medical staff should monitor medical and mental health for signs of deteriorating health.

Because inmates may be assigned to work functions needed to operate a correctional facility, the facility may be adversely affected if inmates participate in a work stoppage. Correctional administrators should employ the same surveillance and response mechanisms as in a food strike. Contingencies, such as bringing in other inmate workers unaffected by the work stoppage, should be considered.

Mass Staff Sick Calls or Staff Strikes

Because correctional facilities have many fixed posts, maintaining minimum staffing levels is critical to sustaining good order in the institution. If staff elect to participate in a mass sick out or "blue flu," facility administrators must be prepared to:

- Remind staff that they are emergency responders and review local labor laws and contract provisions for possible sanctions.

- Activate any reduced staffing plans, such as paring back inmate services and reassigning staff to critical areas

- Activate a recall list, calling in off-duty staff

- Open a dialogue with staff to assess concerns and possible remedies.

Natural or Civil Disasters

Depending upon the geographic location, a correctional facility may be affected by natural disasters such as floods, fires, or storms. Besides activating facility emergency plans, other necessary considerations for correctional staff in these scenarios include:

- If the facility has a generator, the length of time it can run, given the current fuel supply
- Sufficient dry food supplies to supplement meals for long-term kitchen outages
- The possible need to relocate inmates to a nearby facility
- The possibility that more staff may be needed and whether they will need temporary lodging

Housekeeping Plans

A correctional facility must maintain a certain level of environmental standards in accordance to American Correctional Association (ACA) compliance, court-ordered environmental compliance, and/or institutional standards. Because correctional facilities rely on inmates for labor, housekeeping duties usually consist of inmate cadres that are supervised by correctional staff.

Each housing unit has several inmates designated to housekeeping duties, who are responsible for the sanitation of that housing unit. They may also clean common areas of the institution, such as corridors and service areas. These inmates are usually paid a nominal fee as an incentive, which can be spent at the institutional commissary, or inmates may be required to work without compensation as a condition of confinement.

Bomb Plans

As with other emergency plans, each correctional facility maintains a bomb plan. This plan should include:

- A bomb threat card by all the phones that prompts the person who receives the call the necessary questions to ask the caller

- During any bomb threat, the use of radios for communication should be prohibited because they can trigger explosives.

- A notification to police and consideration of the possibility of evacuation.

- A search team should be assembled to look for, but not touch, suspicious packages.

Mass Disturbance Plans

On occasion, based on the size and classification level of a correctional facility, riots or inmate disturbances may transpire. Each facility also maintains a riot disturbance plan that detail the following:

- The required internal and external agency notifications
- The establishment of a command center
- The establishment of a medical triage area, if necessary
- Plans for additional staffing and support from other agencies
- Lockdown procedures to contain the inmate population
- Breaker gate protocols to secure corridors at the facility

- The deployment of reasonable force through chemical agents or other agents of force
- Negotiation tactics and predetermined negotiation teams
- Emergency response teams
- The suspension of non-essential services to deploy staff to the area of the riot

A detailed log of the response should be prepared to document the occurrence. Participants should be maintained on site for the investigation and any subsequent criminal prosecution.

Escape Plans

Because of the probability of an escape, facility escape plans are also maintained for such an event. The plan should address the following:

- Establishing a command post

- Alerting police personnel who have jurisdiction

- Establishing a crime scene at the area of escape

- Commencing a lockdown and a pedigree to confirm the identity of all inmates

- Initiating a search to find evidence of the escape

- Conducting inmate interviews to obtain evidence

- Consideration of suspending non-essential services to deploy extra staff to assist in the search

- Consideration of a media staging area to contain media personnel arriving to the facility

- Beginning a search using resources such as a K-9 patrol

- Reviewing the surveillance cameras to try and determine the escape route

- Notifying the jurisdiction's district attorney, attorneys of record, victims of the escaped inmate, and the media to broadcast a description and photo

Hostage Plans

Each facility maintains a hostage emergency plan. Most correctional facilities have a dedicated hostage negotiation team that trains for such events. Upon notification of the hostage situation, the facility should:

- Activate the hostage emergency plan

- Place the facility on lockdown and contain and control the area of the hostage situation

- Notify the hostage negotiation team

- Try to open a dialogue until the hostage team arrives

- Activate the tactical team for a tactical response, should the hostage negotiation team fail to obtain a successful outcome

- Place the medical team on standby to treat any injuries

Regardless of the rank of the hostage, once captured, the hostage loses authority and the next highest ranked correctional staff takes over.

ACA Standards for Fire Prevention

Correctional facilities are not exempt and must follow all local rules and regulations for fire safety. If a facility is American Correctional Association (ACA) compliant, they will also follow ACA fire safety guidelines. Each facility should have a dedicated fire brigade and conduct drills regularly from established local fire stations in those areas appropriate to respond to the facility. Standards to be monitored include:

- Frequent self-audits and external inspections at predetermined intervals

- Training with external stakeholders to gain a familiarity with the facility

- The use of universally recognized fire safety equipment

- Operable audible and visual detection and alarm systems

- An evacuation plan and transport plan, if needed, with containment areas such as the inmate yard, ready for emergency use

Fire Plans

Correctional facilities maintain fire plans in the control room alongside the other emergency plans. These plans are specific to fire response, and each corrections officer is trained in some level of fire safety. The fire plan consists of designated persons or posts that are part of the fire brigade and who will respond to the fire wagon, don the appropriate gear and equipment, and begin search and rescue. As this is in action that other correctional staff will make, notification to the fire department and other external authorities should proceed as needed.

Emergency response staff also assist with security-related activities to support the fire brigade, such as performing escorts for evacuation, providing security for containment of areas that are unaffected by the fire, and notifying the executive staff and external stakeholders of the facility. Medical staff should also establish a triage area to treat injured persons and consider external notification for ambulance response and to local hospitals, if warranted. A good fire response plan includes rehearsals and drills – both announced and unannounced – at frequent intervals.

Corrections officers and custodial staff should be on the lookout for hazardous conditions that could lead to fire, such as the use and storage of flammable material, the use of cigarettes by staff and inmates, and small rubbish fires, which can spread.

Utility Failure Plans

The facility should have a generator to sustain vital services. Generator tests should be performed monthly and the fuel supply should be determined beforehand to see how long the generator can run without refueling. Other factors to be considered during utility outages are:

- Lighting for safety
- Security systems or gates that may need to be manually operated
- Heat or blankets for warmth in cold weather or ice and water in high temperatures
- Refrigeration, which may be needed for foods and medicines
- Inmates that may be supported by medical devices, which require electricity
- Supplemental dry food provisions in cases of food spoilage

Prison Chaplains

Because the right to practice religion is protected by the constitution, correctional facilities are required to provide religious services to recognized religious groups. This need is usually filled by a paid chaplain in large agencies and may be a volunteer chaplain in a smaller agency. The chaplain works under the facility's program director and may be asked to provide spiritual counseling for inmates of other faiths as well, depending upon need.

Chaplains may perform a ceremonial mass, administer sacraments, or provide counseling to inmates. There are generally schedules of religious services and rules of access. While religious freedoms are protected, religious practice can be modified to prevent anything that might affect the security of the facility.

The chaplains may also be tasked to validate any special religious dietary requests, such as for a Kosher or Halal meal.

Job Positions

There are many functions that take place inside a correctional facility and many job assignments for staff. New officers are generally deployed to inmate housing units on less desirable shifts. As they gain seniority, they can select a more desirable housing unit and a more popular shift. After gaining experience and tenure supervising the inmate population, they can submit and be selected for specialized posts, such as the intake area, clinic, or other support area. They can also be considered for posts in the administrative section of the jail or outside of the jail in a specialized unit, such as transportation, the training academy, central office, or may even be considered for a promotion. A corrections officer is responsible for maintaining security and order in their assigned area.

Corrections Officers' Rights and Duties

The typical corrections officer may be part of a union or, in a non-union state, may be subject to hiring and firing at will. Those officers in a union state are hired under a competitive civil service exam and generally enjoy more labor protections than their non-union counterparts. All correctional staff, regardless of their union status, are protected by universal federal guidelines, such as the Family Medical Leave Act (FMLA), the Fair Standards Act (FLSA), and unemployment protection, including any local labor provisions, as they may relate to overtime, sick leave, or other employee benefits.

The main duties of a correctional officer are care, custody, and control. They are expected to provide the inmate population with all the programs and services that the rules and regulations permit. They must be vigilant and take frequent counts to maintain the custody of inmates under their charge. They have an obligation for inmate care, and if they observe an inmate in need of medical attention or other aid, they are obligated to render it.

Corrections Officers' Responsibilities

As mentioned, corrections officers are responsible for the care, custody, and control of inmates. All correctional staff must display integrity, reliability, and an understanding of the mission and role of the agency. Correctional staff may, at times, be placed in stressful situations and must have the ability to remain calm and rely on their training and institutional policies. They must also be flexible in order to manage mandatory overtime, split shifts, changing shifts, and frequent re-deployment to various job assignments, based on the needs of the facility. The aptitude of corrections staff members should include the ability to write clear, concise, and factual reports.

Corrections Officers' Rights

The federal government provides universal rights to all workers to include correctional staff in all states. Federal protection is provided by the Fair Labor Standards Act (FSLA), which covers minimum standards of employee compensation and the Family Medical Leave Act (FMLA), which covers leave to care for the employee or an immediate family member. All correctional employees are also protected universally by the Americans with Disabilities Act and the Age Discrimination in Employment Act.

In addition to these federal protections, correctional employees can also be protected by state and local employment guidelines. Examples are New York City's law, which provides employees in that region five paid sick days per year, or California's Labor Law, which provides California residents overtime pay after eight hours of work in a day. In addition to federal, state, and local protections, the employee in a union state may also be protected by the provisions of a collective bargaining agreement. If so, the employee has the rights to due process among other benefits, to further protect their employment.

Code of Ethics

Because correctional staffs are in positions of public trust, their ethics must be beyond reproach. They are granted broad authority and power and therefore, can be challenged to accept bribes, smuggle contraband, or face other ethical dilemmas.

Ethics is a morale code of doing what is right and lawful. Ethics involves a value system and standards of conduct. Ethical guidelines can vary based upon jurisdiction. Each correctional agency has a written code of ethics and values and offers training and guidance for correctional staff.

Ethical Principles

Ethical principles are part of the correctional agency's policy and part of the recruiting and in-service training programs. The code of ethics should be conspicuously posted in the facility and constantly reinforced. Good ethical behavior should be recognized and rewarded. The code of ethics mandates:

- Maintaining a certain level of professionalism both on and off duty
- Following all rules, polices, and procedures, regardless of the corrections officer's own beliefs
- Reporting all policy violations and any suspected criminal wrongdoings
- Prohibiting the acceptance of gifts or gratuities

- Maintaining confidentiality, when required
- Avoiding shortcuts in policy and procedures
- Prohibiting discrimination, punitive behavior, or retaliation

Unethical Behaviors

Corrections officers may be challenged with many ethical dilemmas. When confronted with ethical dilemmas, they must be guided by the agency's ethics policy in conjunction with agency rules and regulations. When in doubt about a possible ethical situation, the officer should seek guidance from a supervisor, the agency's ethics board, or legal division. Some of the ethical challenges correctional staff may face include:

- Becoming too familiar with inmates or visitors
- Accepting small gifts or favors from inmates or their families
- Using an inmate as an enforcer, over other inmates, to keep a shift quiet
- Being pressured to smuggle contraband
- The desire to abuse or retaliate against inmates
- Engaging in off-duty activity that would discredit the agency
- Failing to report rule violations that may get the employee or colleagues in trouble

Recognizing Unethical Behavior

Indications of unethical behavior are not always clear or easy to recognize. However, there are some high-risk behaviors that may be indicative of unethical behavior including:

- Someone who may be experiencing financial problems

- Someone who is overly friendly or flirtatious with inmates or who spends time with inmates isolated away from other staff

- Someone who is the subject of one or more complaints

- Someone who is under frequent stress or that may be facing problems outside of work such as illness, financial burden, or other factors that may affect their judgment.

Any employee witnessing unethical behavior has an obligation to report it. If it involves something of a clear criminal nature, the officer should immediately report it to the agency's inspector general, office of integrity, or local police. If the violation is of a non-criminal nature, the officer should immediately report it to a supervisor. To maintain confidentiality, some agencies provide a confidential outlet for staff and inmates to report wrongdoings, to protect the identity of the person reporting.

Code of Silence

The *code of silence* or the *blue wall of silence* are phrases used to describe when officers do not report wrongdoings, in an effort to protect other correctional staff members. To combat the code of silence, the agency's culture should protect staff who speak out; publishing a clear code of ethics is a good starting place. Correctional facilities can also educate on compliance through training, frequent tests, and audits. Staff should also be provided multiple outlets and avenues to report corruption – both overtly and covertly. Continual ethics training should reinforce the agency's ethical mission and goals.

Corrections officers take an oath of office and should never feel pressured to maintain a code of silence. The main duty of correctional staff is to carry out their duties without bias and immediately report any wrongdoing, regardless of who is involved.

Supervisors' Duties

Supervisors are the backbone of any correctional facility. They are the first line of supervision, responsible for the enforcement of rules and regulations. Supervisors must be trainers and educators while conducting in-service training for their subordinates. They must diffuse confrontational situations and develop resolutions to problems they encounter during their supervision tenure. They must review schedules, ensure that policies and procedures are followed, and must communicate between divisions and units of the agency to maintain good order. Supervisors must also review and investigate complaints while initiating disciplinary action, if needed.

Supervisors must receive more training than the line staff they supervise. They must review paperwork, written reports, and log entries written by corrections officers. Supervisors must verbally test staff knowledge of policies and procedures. Oftentimes, supervisors will be called upon as emergency responders and will be responsible to establish crimes scenes, direct medical responses, and guide the officers in emergency management.

Chain of Command

A chain of command is a strict method of command modeled after military organizations, in which the lowest level staff report up to the highest ranking in defined hierarchy order. In a correctional facility, the officers are the line staff who report up to the supervisors, who are considered the first line of supervision. The first line supervisors then report up to the shift commanders, who are considered the second line of supervision and the reporting continues up the chain to the warden or superintendent of the facility. Those in the chain of command do not go around the chain; line officers do not report directly to the warden. This system permits strict accountability and prevents ambiguity in the flow of information and span of control.

Firearms

Because correctional officers are responsible for the care, custody, and control of inmates, they may be assigned to staff a post that requires a firearm. A post, such as a perimeter or tower post, may require that the officer utilize a longer-ranged weapon, such as a rifle. Conversely, a post such as escorting a prisoner to a hospital may require that the corrections officer utilize a pistol-type weapon.

Officers receive weapons training in the use of the firearms and are required to demonstrate a certain level of proficiency. Some states are governed by peace officer statutes, which determine the length and type of firearms training required.

Not all corrections officers are assigned firearms. Assignment depends upon their certification, the needs of the facility, and the post or function they are assigned to. All institutional firearms are kept secure in the facility's arsenal, which can be in the control room or sally port area of the facility. No firearms are permitted inside the facility where inmates are housed, except in the possible rare instance when a contraband firearm is suspected to be in the facility and a ballistic search is ordered. A ballistic search is when the special correctional operations team locks down the facility and searches each unit and inmate at gunpoint, in the pursuit of the contraband firearm among the inmate population.

Since the use of firearms is considered lethal force, their use is also governed by state and local laws, in addition to agency rules and regulations.

Pat-Down Search Procedures

Because of the constant need to prevent the introduction and movement of contraband within correctional facilities, pat-downs are a useful search method. A pat-down requires the inmate to first empty their pockets of belongings. Next, they are ordered to stand facing the wall with their hands above their head and feet shoulder-width apart. The officer then run his or her hands along the inmate's clothing and body outline to feel for any contraband. When this is completed, the officer will ask the inmate to turn and face forward while opening his or her mouth and sticking out the tongue, to make sure the inmate is not hiding any contraband in their oral cavity. If the inmate has hair that is difficult to see though, the officer will ask the inmate to run their fingers through their hair.

A pat-down search is different than a strip search, in which the inmate is asked to remove all their clothing. In a strip search, there is no contact between the inmate and the officer because visual inspection can easily reveal the presence of any contraband. Pat-down searches are generally conducted when the inmate is moving between areas within the institution, while a strip search is reserved for inmates entering and leaving the confines of the facility. Federal law currently prohibits the use of strip searches for detainee prisoners convicted of misdemeanor offenses.

Inmate Intake Procedures

The holding area where inmates enter and exit the correctional facility is known as the intake area. In the intake area, the inmate is identified through fingerprints. After verifying the inmate's identity, the inmate is sent for medical testing and evaluated for mental health issues. Inmates are also given a new admission orientation to familiarize them with the facility and institutional policies. Inmates are provided with a copy of the rules and regulations of the facility and must sign for them. Next, inmates are asked a series of questions in a process known as *classification*, where the inmate is considered for housing placement. Housing placement is decided based upon gender, age, criminal charges, or history, among other factors. Once the classification process is complete, the inmate is given a classification score and be housed with inmates with similar classification scores. The placement designation might also be superseded by special medical or mental health housing needs, regardless of the classification score, to give the inmate acute medical or mental health care.

While in the intake area, inmates will be issued a photo identification card. The legal documents or writ of detainer are reviewed. In the intake area, inmates will be afforded access to the telephone and shower, and are given personal hygiene items along with an institutional uniform.

Newly admitted prisoners do not always go directly to the housing unit that their classification score dictates. They may first be placed in a new admission area for observation for the manifestation of any communicable diseases, such as tuberculosis. Before placing inmates in general population units, some facilities may incubate them in new admission housing units for several days, pending the results of medical testing, to limit the spread of communicable disease.

Pre-Service and In-Service Training

Because corrections officers face a myriad of challenges with the population they serve, they receive extensive training on broad topics including ethics, law, suicide prevention, and firearm training. A new recruit officer will receive training through an academy before being assigned to a facility. This training is known as *pre-service training*.

After an officer is initially trained and subsequently assigned to a command, they require yearly training to keep current in their skills and learn new skills not received in pre-service training. This subsequent training is known as *in-service training* and is required for the officer to maintain certification. In many instances, in-service training is also applicable to supervisors.

In addition to pre-service and in-service training, some officers may also receive specialized training. For example, staff members working in mental health areas may get enhanced training to deal with special populations, or those working in punitive segregation areas may get specialized training in the use of force.

Occupational Stress

Multiple studies have determined that corrections officers encounter a great deal of stress in the workplace. The stress comes from working with a challenging population, exposure to shift work, and exposure to large amounts of overtime, among other factors. If left untreated, stress can lead to medical and mental health problems and possibly even suicide.

As a result, many facilities encourage employee wellness and maintain programs for recognizing symptomatic staff. Some agencies have employment assistance programs (EAP) to help staff navigate through challenging or stressful situations. Providing outlets for staff to channel and relieve their stress will help maintain the good order of the facility.

Some larger correctional agencies have enough resources to provide critical incident staff with debriefing teams, which have specially trained staff to help corrections officers cope, after they are involved in traumatic events.

Sexual Harassment

Federal, state, and local laws protect all persons against sexual harassment. Correctional facilities must also abide by the protections afforded by these laws. In addition to mandated governmental regulations, the correctional agency will also have rules and policies that govern sexual harassment and sexual discrimination. Violations can result in discipline ranging from a reprimand to termination. Staff can also be held personally liable for their actions and may be subject to a lawsuit, where the agency will not indemnify them if the offense is considered outside the employee's scope of employment.

Sexual discrimination involves providing unequal rights to a person based upon their gender. Sexual harassment takes the form of unwanted sexual advances or commenting on sexuality in a vulgar or unsolicited way. It should be noted that once an employee makes a complaint of sexual discrimination or harassment, any further negative action by the employer may be viewed as retaliatory and be penalized worse than the original reported offense.

Security Classifications

As mentioned, inmates are categorized and separated within the facility utilizing a scoring system known as *classification*. Inmates are separated first by gender, with males going to one location and females to another. If space permits, female prisoners are placed in an entirely separate institution than males. The next classification separation is done by age, in which adults go to one location and adolescents another.

Within the subsets of gender and age, corrections staff further identify more subsets of minimum-security, medium-security, and so on, to place inmates in housing units with like individuals. This ensures that the inmates are placed in an area that supports their needs and the needs of the facility, and helps ensure that more aggressive inmates don't prey on weaker inmates.

In the classification process, inmates receive a score based upon criteria such as their age, criminal history, violent crime history, and gang affiliation. Those with no prior criminal history and no violent crimes are given a lower score, while the highest scores are reserved for the most violent inmates.

There are several exceptions to the classification process, such as inmates with medical or mental health needs, inmates with a high risk of harm due the nature of their charge, or inmates who are notorious and may be the target of other inmates. Some facilities may also elect to isolate gangs as part of their security strategy. That gang strategy may depend on how many gang members are in the facility and what security challenges they pose to the facility. The decision involving gang member placement is usually decided by the deputy warden of security and approved by the warden or superintendent.

Basic Cell Rendering

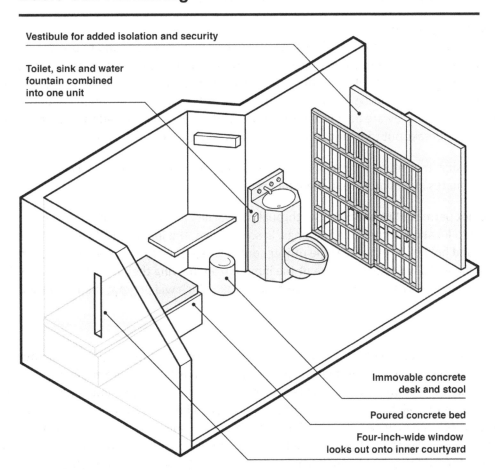

Vestibule for added isolation and security

Toilet, sink and water fountain combined into one unit

Immovable concrete desk and stool

Poured concrete bed

Four-inch-wide window looks out onto inner courtyard

Minimum-Security Facilities

Non-violent inmates who are serving short sentences with a low risk of escape are housed in minimum-security level facilities. The non-violent inmates are generally housed in a barracks-type environment without cells and have more freedom of movement around the facility and less supervision than higher classification facilities. Minimum-security facilities typically do not have the high razor ribbon fences that surround higher classification facilities and may not even have a wall or fence at all. An escape at a minimum-security facility might involve a low classification prisoner walking off the property or not returning to the facility from a community day program when required. This type of escape is referred to as a *walk off.*

Medium-Security Facilities

Medium-security facilities house a population of inmates who may have a classification too high to be considered for a low classification facility, but not high enough to merit placement in the most restrictive maximum-security facilities. Medium-security facility housing units have a mix of cells and dormitories. The inmates may move between cell and dorm units as their classification gets higher or lower. Inmates in medium-security facilities have certain freedoms and liberties but not as much as those in minimum-security facilities. Medium-security facility have a secure perimeter and escorted movement for the population who have a higher classification.

Maximum-Security Facilities

Maximum-security facilities have the highest levels of security restrictions and house some of the agency's most violent offenders. Many more security precautions are taken to manage this population. This includes a more secure facility with the most advanced technology the agency has, along with an infrastructure of only cell housing units to be able secure individual inmates when needed. Some inmate cells are so secure that they are built inside the prison without being attached to an exterior wall, so that if the inmate breaks out of their cell, they are still within the confines of the facility.

Generally speaking, maximum-security inmates are serving long sentences and have a higher risk of escape than inmates in minimum- and medium-security facilities.

Inmates are not permitted free movement through the facility and in most cases, they require an escort from location to location in controlled settings. In some cases, the inmates will be handcuffed while out of their cells and held by a tether that the officer controls. Leg irons can also be placed on the inmate to prevent running and a waist belt to prevent the inmate from moving their hands away from their waist. In severe cases, inmates can be forced to don a spit mask, which will prevent them from spitting on staff.

Supermax Facilities

Supermax is the highest level of security classification and is reserved for dangerous inmates, generally with well-established behavioral problems. Inmates in supermax facilities are confined to their cells twenty-three hours a day with food coming to the cell through a slot in the door. They are only permitted outside the cell for one hour a day for recreation, where they will be in a single enclosed recreation yard cell and may be handcuffed during the session. Inmate showers take place in the cell, along with services delivered to the cell via a television monitor. Visits, if permitted, are restricted more than what is afforded for general population inmates and will be without visitor physical contact. Mail or communication for the inmate may be restricted or even prohibited by court order. These severe protections are taken to keep both the officer and inmate safe. The level of staff supervision is much greater in supermax facilities than in lower classification level facilities.

Security Measures

The higher the classification level of the facility, the more inaccessible the facility will be, to help prevent escape. High classification facilities, like the infamous and now closed Alcatraz Federal Prison, could be only accessed by boat. High classification facilities have several fences with electronic detection systems, which contain *shaker alarms* to notify staff if the fence is shaken. They will also have *intrusion zones* to alert staff if someone walks in the sterile area. The fences around maximum-security facilities can also be electrified and shrouded in razor ribbon embedded into fences. Fences in high-security facilities have six feet of cement under them to prohibit tunneling, while low-classification facilities might not have fences at all. High security facilities may also have armed tower guards or outside patrols to prevent escape.

Some lower classification housing facilities may be simple tents or temporary structures, while secure facilities are brick and mortar with high walls, multiple fences, and maintain high levels of supervision. New York City places its inmate population on Ryker's Island, which is surrounded by dangerous waters and is only accessible by a single bridge. This prevents the likelihood of an easy escape, because inmates breaking out of a facility would still have to swim off the island or traverse a well-guarded bridge. Many correctional agencies take advantage of natural barriers to further challenge an easy escape attempt.

Sally Ports

A *sally port* is an area enclosed by two gates within a correctional facility. It can be used to permit vehicle access at an entrance to the facility or for inmate movement inside a facility to move prisoners from one location to another. The principle behind the sally port is that the persons or vehicles enter the sally port from the furthest door or gate, which is then shut behind them. This permits the correction staff to examine the vehicle or persons in a secure room. The officer knows that no one else can sneak in or out while that vehicle or inmates are secure in the sally port. The officer can then inspect the under carriage of the vehicle, and ask staff or inmates for their identification in a controlled environment. Once the officer is satisfied with the verification of the persons or vehicles in the sally port, they can open the door of the sally port and permit final access or egress. Sally ports are an enhanced method to control movement.

While vehicles are in sally ports, corrections officers can use mirrors to look for contraband under vehicles or for inmates hiding under transport vehicles. In higher classification facilities, all vehicles departing the facility are searched for inmates who might attempt escape.

A Sally Port

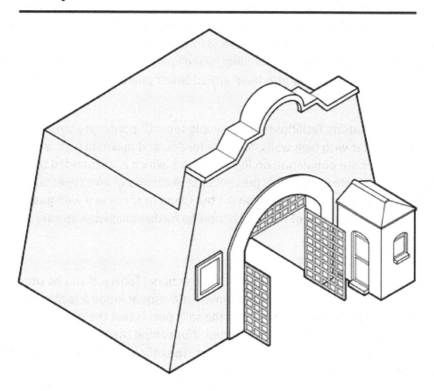

Control Centers and Safety Vestibules

The *control center* or *control room* is the main operations center of the facility. It is normally located near the facility's entrance and has a control room supervisor who maintains communication with all the individual units of the facility. The control center maintains all the facility's emergency plans, munitions, radios, and emergency equipment. The control center is also responsible of making notifications to both internal staff and external agencies, if needed. The control center is considered the most vital part of the facility and where schedules of staffing, facilities keys, and fire safety equipment are kept. It is also where calls for assistance from staff are received and where emergency responses are dispatched. It is often referred to as the "brain" of the facility, where all operational functions originate.

A safety vestibule is an area that can be blocked off in both directions by an electronic or manual gate, to prohibit inmate access through either side, especially useful in facility emergencies. It prevents the spread of inmates if they escape from another area of the facility and serves to contain them while keeping staff safe.

Writ of Detainer

In many instances, while prisoners are incarcerated in one facility, another agency may also want them for a crime that occurred in their jurisdiction. In order to claim their right to the prisoner, they may seek a court order to issue a notice to the holding facility that they are a wanting authority and seek

152

detention of the inmate as well. The court will then issue a *writ of detainer*, which may also be issued to notify the holding agency to make notifications when that inmate is about to be released from custody. All court orders should be processed by the facility's general office, where staff have experience interpreting court orders and documents.

Felonies and Misdemeanors

Criminal offenses fall into two categories: misdemeanors or felonies. Misdemeanors are lower level offenses such as petty theft or drinking in public that can be handled with penalties, ranging from a fine to up to one year in jail.

Felonies, by contrast, are more serious offenses, such as a robbery or assault, and can result in long sentences and serious consequences. Suspects charged with serious felonies can be kept in jail without chance of bail until the criminal case has concluded in the courts.

Individuals in custody as detainees, but not yet sentenced, are permitted the right to vote. In most states, once convicted, a prisoner loses the right to vote while in prison and may lose the right to vote permanently, depending upon the local and state laws in which they reside.

Probation and Parole

Probation and parole are both forms of community corrections in which an offender is supervised in a street environment. The main distinction between the two is that probation is pre-incarceration and parole is post-conviction. An individual convicted of a crime may be given probation in lieu of incarceration. Their supervision takes place in the community, where they have to follow the rules of their probation, which may include checking in with their probation officer, maintaining gainful employment, and successfully passing drug tests. If they fail to meet conditions of their probation, they can be placed in jail.

By contrast, parole allows sentenced individuals out in the street under correctional supervision before their full sentence is complete. This is generally reserved for a prisoner who has served some prison time and has exhibited good enough behavior for the parole board to endorse his or her release. Probation is decided by the sentencing judge after a pre-sentence investigation is conducted to gather background information on the individual charged. The judge usually wants to see if the person has employment and housing, and what benefits a probation might pose to the individual.

Parole is usually decided by a board of individuals who sit on the parole board. The inmate's institutional behavior, along with evidence of any reform he or she may have achieved, is reviewed by the board when in consideration of an early release. If the parole is granted, the person still remains on correctional supervision in the community until the time that their sentence would have been complete.

Nolle Prosequi and Nolo Contendere

Nolle prosequi is the term to describe when the prosecutor in a criminal case declines to pursue a conviction. A common reason a prosecutor may choose this strategy is when the individual being charged by that prosecutor is also being charged by another prosecutor in the same state, but in a different jurisdiction, for the same charge. One prosecutor may elect to invoke *Nolle prosequi* in order to avoid double jeopardy.

Nolo contendere is the term used to describe the defense of the person being charged, in which they plead *Nolo contendere* or "no contest." This means that they do not wish to fight the charges but are not admitting guilt. Sentencing will still transpire and the purpose of this defense is for the defendant to accept the criminal sentence but deny guilt, in order to defend a possible civil lawsuit.

Adjudication

Adjudication is the term used by the court to indicate that a determination has been made in a court action. Possible adjudication outcomes include:

- A conviction, where the individual is found guilty
- An acquittal, where the individual is cleared of wrongdoing
- A dismissal, when it is determined there is not enough evidence to proceed

In some cases, the adjudication can be delayed or adjourned contemplating dismissal if the offender does not get charged again within a predetermined period of time. After this time, the conviction is erased or sealed with no further action.

Expunction and Deferred Adjudication

Expunction, also called *expungement*, is the removal of the record of criminal charges after an individual has been sentenced. Expunction is most commonly used for minors to permit their juvenile record from impeding them from employment later in life. With expunction, if the individual does not have another encounter with the criminal justice system within a predetermined amount of time, the records can be sealed to the general public.

Deferred adjudication is where the sentencing body does not follow through with the proceedings or discipline which they hold in suspense, unless another criminal act is committed by the offender, which will then trigger a resumption of the original charges previously held in abeyance.

Sentencing Guidelines

In response to rising national crimes rates and the belief that judges were being too lenient with sentencing, sentencing guidelines were created. Sentencing guidelines provide a range of penalties for federal and some local state judges for deviations. These guidelines resulted in a lack of judicial discretion to permit lenient sentences where applicable, resulting in longer prison sentences.

In the wake of decreasing national crime rates, current national trends have seen softening of harsh sentencing guidelines. Those who oppose sentencing guidelines argue that they do not permit judges to consider mitigating circumstances in criminal cases, which would otherwise permit them to grant softer sentences where warranted.

Determinate and Indeterminate Sentences

Offenders can be sentenced to either determinate or indeterminate sentences. A *determinate sentence* is a sentence in which the judge specifies a specific length of time, such as a five-year sentence. The prisoner must serve the full five years of their sentence before being released.

An *indeterminate sentence* is a sentence not yet determined. An example would be an offender sentenced to five to fifteen years. That would mean he or she would have to serve a minimum of five years before being considered for parole, but in no case, will the offender serve more than fifteen years, which is the expiration of the sentence. The sentence is considered indeterminate because the actual length of the sentence is not fully determined at sentencing. Instead, it is decided at the correctional facility based upon several factors, including the inmate's behavior at the facility and any reform efforts.

Concurrent and Consecutive Sentences

Inmates may be charged with multiple offenses at the same time. Depending on their sentence, they can serve those sentences either concurrently or consecutively. With concurrent sentences, the inmate can serve both sentences simultaneously, thereby reducing his or her time of incarceration. If the sentences are served consecutively, then one of the sentences must be completed before the other starts, which results in a longer incarceration.

For example, an inmate sentenced to consecutive sentences of one year for one case and one year on another case would end up serving two full years. If the same inmate was sentenced to concurrent sentences on two cases of one year each, the inmate would only end up serving one year.

Protective Custody

Protective custody is reserved for inmates who may be at risk or harm in general population housing units. Protective custody may be reserved for former law enforcement or governmental officials, for inmates charged with high profile crimes or sexual offenses, or inmates who were the victims of jail violence.

It is the facility's responsibility to keep all inmates safe. Segregating inmates into protective custody who are at high risk of harm, limits the possibility of assault. Within protective custody, there may be further categories of subsets or segregation set up to keep protective custody inmates safe from each other.

Good time

Good time is a term used to describe a reduction in sentence length for an inmate. Some sentences are not eligible for good time and some jurisdictions do not provide good time, but these cases are the exception, not the norm. Most jurisdictions allow an inmate good time to permit a reduced sentence as an incentive for good behavior. This reduction can be as much as one third off the sentence.

In some cases, the good time is automatically given to the inmates, unless it is taken away through the discipline process. In other cases, the inmate must earn good time by participating in work and other programming to merit the decreased sentence. Those serving life sentences are not eligible for good time or a reduction in their sentence.

Honor blocks

Honor blocks are a preferred housing option for inmates who have maintained good behavior in the facility. It is an incentive for increased benefits for the inmate to strive for. Privileges can include coveted work assignments or more time out of the cell, among other privileges. The continued incentive is to remain with good behavior or the privileges may be lost with deviant behavior.

Counts

Inmates in a correction facility are counted frequently to prevent and detect escape. There are a variety of counts to include pedigree counts, standing counts, formal counts, and informal counts. A formal count is conducted at a predetermined time, such as shift changes, and requires the counting of a breathing body with evident signs of life. Informal counts are taken at frequent intervals throughout the tour, but no less than every half hour. Pedigree counts are where the inmate is not only counted as a body, but their identity is also verified through a photo and other personal information. Standing counts are where the inmates must line up and be counted while vertical.

All these forms of counts permit the correctional staff to physically observe the inmate to ensure no unreported trauma is visible on his or her body. Counting is one of the most critical functions in any correctional facility and is paramount to maintaining accurate track of inmates' presence and to detect escape. It is critical that when corrections officers perform a count that they physically see signs of life of the inmate being counted, such as the chest rising and falling during sleeping. Some inmates may commit suicide, which could go undetected without the officer observing signs of life. Other inmates might escape and leave they shape of a body in clothing, which may fool the officer. It is for this reason that observing signs of life is important to make ensure the inmate has not fooled the officer.

Practice Questions

1. Which of the following are examples of community corrections?
    I. A person incarcerated in jail
    II. A person incarcerated in prison
    III. A person on probation
    a. II and III
    b. I and III
    c. I and II
    d. I, II, and III

2. According to the Bureau of Justice statistics, how many people are currently incarcerated in the United States?
    a. Approximately 100,000
    b. Approximately 2 million
    c. Over 14 million
    d. The exact number has not been estimated

3. Of the incarcerated population in the United States, approximately what percentage is female?
    a. Under 2%
    b. 6 to 8%
    c. 35%
    d. Slightly less than 50%

4. What correctional organization was the first to develop a set of standards and audits to measure the quality and performance at correctional institutions?
    a. The American Correctional Association (ACA)
    b. The National Institute of Corrections (NIC)
    c. The National Commission on Correctional Healthcare (NCCHC)
    d. The Prison Rape Elimination Act (PREA)

5. Which of the following provides federal guidelines as a result of federal legislation passed in 2003 that guides the reporting and monitoring of sexual assault in U.S. jails and prisons?
    a. The American Correction Association Act (ACA) of 2003
    b. The Prison Rape Elimination Act (PREA)
    c. The Affordable Care Act (ACA)
    d. None of the above

6. What country incarcerates more prisoners than any other nation?
    a. Russia
    b. China
    c. The United States
    d. North Korea

7. Which of the following is true regarding the juvenile populations in correction institutions?

    a. Since they are the youngest, they are the easiest to manage.

    b. All juveniles will either get sentenced to probation or to a juvenile detention facility.

    c. Juveniles are a difficult population to manage because of the need to supply state-mandated school programs.

    d. Juvenile prisoners will not be placed in a correction facility and are part of the juvenile detention system.

8. Which early correctional philosophy took root from the Quakers and put a heavy emphasis on solitary confinement?

    a. The Pennsylvania system

    b. The Auburn System

    c. The Arizona system

    d. The isolation system

9. Which of the following is the best example of direct supervision?

    a. An officer in a control station watching housing area inmates on a monitor

    b. An officer supervising inmates in a housing unit

    c. A perimeter officer at the correction institution

    d. None of the above provides a good example of direct supervision

10. Which of the following examples best describes the unit management approach?

    a. A warden supervising the chain of command

    b. A jail or prison split up into mini units of supervision

    c. Each jail or prison is considered a unit of the overall agency

    d. A supervisor assigned to supervise officers in each housing unit

11. Which of the following is the LEAST effective way to communicate facility polices to inmates?

    a. As part of the new admission orientation process

    b. Through signage posted at the facility

    c. As part of the discipline process

    d. Having the inmate sign for the copy of the facility rules and regulations

12. Which of the following should correctional staff NOT do during a bomb threat?

    a. Notify police

    b. Consider evacuation

    c. Notify all staff via radio of the existence of the bomb threat

    d. Ask the caller questions about the bomb threat from a questionnaire

13. In reference to a facility hostage plan, once the staff member is taken hostage, which of the following is true?

    a. They lose all authority regardless of their rank

    b. They retain full authority

    c. An election must be held to choose a replacement for the staff member

    d. They temporarily lose rank, but maintain authority

14. In reference to corrections officers' rights, which of the following is NOT a federal right?
    a. The Fair Labor Standards Act
    b. The Family Medical Leave Act
    c. State workers' compensation
    d. The Americans with Disabilities Act

15. What is the location inside a correctional institution where inmates process in and out of the facility called?
    a. The sally port
    b. The control room
    c. The intake area
    d. The processing room

16. While it is not always easy to spot unethical behavior, which of the following may be a warning sign of unethical behavior?
    a. Someone who seems too perfect
    b. Someone who has a financial hardship
    c. Someone who is always happy
    d. There are no warning signs for unethical behavior so all people are suspect.

17. Which of the following is the best example of an in-service training?
    a. Training a new recruit
    b. Annual recertification for an existing corrections officer
    c. Training required as part of entry into a specialized unit
    d. None of the above is a good example of in-service training

18. In reference to sexual harassment, retaliation can sometimes be which of the following?
    a. Penalized worse than the original offense
    b. An effective deterrent to false claims
    c. Accepted as an understandable response
    d. Taken as proof of guilt

19. What is the main purpose of a sally port?
    a. To pedigree inmates entering the facility for the first time
    b. To process inmates in and out of a jail
    c. To contain persons and vehicles in a secure area for compartmentalization, verification and safe passage to the next area
    d. To prevent inmates from escaping from the facility

20. What area best describes the correctional facility's operations center?
    a. The control center
    b. The intake area
    c. The sally port
    d. The general office

21. Which of the following best describes a writ of detainer?
    a. A court order sentencing the inmate
    b. A court order requesting that the facility hold custody of the inmate for another jurisdiction or to notify that jurisdiction of pending release
    c. A court order to notify the victims of the crime upon release of the inmate from the facility
    d. A court order identifying the inmate's bail conditions

22. In reference to misdemeanors and felonies, which of the following statements is most accurate?
    a. Persons charged with misdemeanors cannot receive jail time
    b. Felonies are more serious crimes than misdemeanors
    c. Misdemeanors are more serious crimes than felonies
    d. People charged with felonies cannot receive jail time

23. What is the main difference between probation and parole?
    a. Probation is served before prison time while parole is served after serving prison time
    b. Parole is served before prison time while probation is served after serving prison time
    c. Probation is considered by the parole board while parole is ordered by a judge
    d. The only difference between probation and parole is the type of supervision

24. Which of the following statements is most accurate in reference to concurrent and consecutive sentences?
    a. Concurrent sentences are served at the same time, resulting in a shorter incarceration time for the individual
    b. Concurrent sentences are served one after another, resulting in a longer incarceration time.
    c. Consecutive sentences are served at the same time, resulting in shorter incarceration times.
    d. Consecutive sentences can be served at two different correctional facilities.

25. Which of the following criteria is NOT considered in regards to inmate classification?
    a. Age
    b. Race
    c. Criminal history
    d. Any past institutional violence history

Answer Explanations

1. C: Community corrections is when a person is not kept inside a correctional facility, such as in Choices *A* or *B*, but monitored while they are allowed to live in a regular environment with various sets of restrictions. Some of these situations include being granted probation or parole, transition to a halfway house or day reporting center, or being part of a community-based program such as a work release program.

2. B: It is estimated that there are over 2 million individuals in facilities such as jails and prisons in the United States. In addition, there are another 6 million placed in some type of community corrections, such as probation, parole, or community programs. The other choices are well above or below the acknowledged estimates.

3. B: It is estimated that about 6-8% of the incarcerated population is female. This female population is increasing faster than the male population, due to substance abuse issues in the female population. Minorities accused or convicted of non-violent, narcotics-related crimes make up the majority of incarcerated females.

4. A: One of the earliest correctional organizations with this goal was the American Correctional Association (ACA), originating in the 1800's. The NIC came nearly a century later and is a federal agency. The NCCHC is concerned more specifically with health issues in correctional facilities. The PREA is legislation dealing with that particular issue in such facilities.

5. B: The Prison Rape Elimination Act (PREA) is the federal law concerned with these matters in correctional facilities. The ACA (American Correction Association) is the association concerned with general standards for facilities. It is not an act like the rest of the choices. The ACA is concerned with healthcare coverage for the general population.

6. C: The United States openly acknowledges the number of people that are incarcerated and in community corrections situations. The United States has the highest percentage of incarcerated individuals, with about two million incarcerated. In addition, there are about six million persons in the U.S. that are serving some type of community correction sentence.

7. C: The added need for specialized programs for juveniles, such as school programs that meet state approval, is one challenge with managing the juvenile population in a correctional facility. Younger individuals also demonstrate a greater tendency toward criminal behavior, so Choice *A* is unlikely. Choice *B* does not really reveal anything about the juvenile population in correctional facilities. Choice *D* is not necessarily true, as a state's juvenile detention system may include correctional facilities of some type.

8. A: The Pennsylvania system was initially used as a model system based on the Quaker thinking that confinement in solitary isolation tends to reform a person more than group containment. After criticism of the Pennsylvania system's results, the Auburn system (named after a facility in New York) replaced this system. Systems referred to as Arizona or isolation systems were not discussed.

9. B: Direct supervision occurs when an officer directly patrols and observes the areas where inmates are kept. Choice *A* is incorrect because supervision is through a monitor and the officer is somewhere at a distance from the actual inmates. Choice *C* involves an officer who patrols and observes the outer boundary of a facility to prevent escape, but is not directly patrolling or observing where the inmates are supposed to be.

10. B: The unit management method breaks down the facility into smaller units. For each of these smaller units, there is a team that focuses on that unit. Facility-wide rules and policies still apply, but having the same staff focused on the same mini-unit allows for better familiarity with those incarcerated and that part of the facility. This can possibly lead to safer operations. The other choices do not refer to what this method actually entails.

11. C: Communicating a policy to an inmate after he or she has committed an infraction is too late. There are several ways to disseminate information regarding facility policy rules and regulations to the inmates. Some of those methods include the new admission process at orientation, through signage, at service areas and housing units, and through counselors. Inmates can also review a facility's rules and policies at its law library.

12. C: Radios should not be used if there is a bomb threat because radio use can set off some types of explosives. Police should be notified, evacuation should be considered, and the person receiving the threat should try to ask the caller for as much relevant information as possible to help the bomb investigation. Therefore, there are often prompting cards placed by phones to remind staff what to ask.

13. A: If one of the staff is taken hostage, regardless of rank, that staff member's authority is no longer in effect while being held captive. The staff member next in rank in that area of authority will temporarily take on the captive staff member's authority. Rank is irrelevant to the plan here, and the plan already contains provision to replace the staff member with the next officer in line, without the need for elections or other decision-making mechanisms, as there likely is not time for those.

14. C: State workers' compensation is a state-administered plan. The other three legislative acts are all federal mandates. The federal ones cover all workers nationally, while each state's plan provides additional protections and rights to that state's workers. There may be additional plans administered by local jurisdictions or the facility itself.

15. C: The area where new inmates come into the jail is known as the intake area. In this area, inmates' identities are confirmed through fingerprints and they are processed for medical and mental health status checks to identify any issues. Inmates receive new admission orientation as well as the rules and regulations of the facility. In this way, they can begin to become familiar with the facility and the policies. The other choices serve different purposes in the facility.

16. B: A person having financial struggles may be at increased risk of unethical behavior. An appearance of being too perfect is not one of the signs associated with possible unethical behavior. Happiness is also not necessarily a sign that unethical behavior is occurring. There are some other signs that can indicate the possibility of unethical behavior, particular closeness with inmates, receiving complaints, and signs of stress.

17. B: The best example listed here is a type of yearly training to recertify corrections credentials. Choice *A* is an example of pre-service training because it is for a new recruit and not a current officer. Choice *C* involves specialized training for a special purpose (so neither pre-service nor in-service in particular), such as a one-time training needed to become part of a special unit.

18. A: It is possible that a form of retaliation or action that could be seen as retaliation can draw more severe punishment than the original act in question itself. Such retaliatory action will not be considered as a deterrent or understandable, so Choices *B* and *C* are not viable. It is also not necessarily taken as a sign of guilt, so Choice *D* is not a good answer.

19. C: A sally port provides an area where persons and vehicles that are to move from one area to another can be held temporarily in isolation to be more securely inspected and challenged. Therefore, Choice *C* is the best answer. Other better equipped areas can be designated to pedigree inmates, so Choice *A* is not the best option. A dedicated intake area is best to process inmates in and out of a correctional facility, so Choice *B* is incorrect. Preventing escape may be one purpose of a sally port, but it is also the purpose of many parts of a correctional facility, so Choice *D* is not the best option.

20. A: The term *control center* is synonymous with the *operations center* of the facility. The intake area is specifically for processing inmates in and out of a facility, so Choice *B* is incorrect. A sally port is specifically to make one transit location more secure, so Choice *C* is not correct. The general office has more administrative purposes therefore, choice D is not correct. The control center is somewhat akin to a "brain" – a location where important communication enters and leaves.

21. B: A writ of detainer is an order obtained from a court to get a facility to hold an inmate about to be released or to give notice that the inmate is about to be released to another agency that may also have charges to file against the inmate. It does not involve sentencing, so Choice *A* is not correct. It is to notify an agency – not victims – so Choice *C* is incorrect. It is not specifically about determining bail conditions, so Choice *D* is not the best option.

22. B: Felonies are more serious crimes and therefore, they carry more serious sentences than misdemeanors. Those charged with a misdemeanor may end up serving some time in jail, but not prison, so Choice *A* is incorrect. Choice *C* reversed the relationship between the two, so it is not correct. Those charged with felonies may serve some of their initial time in jail awaiting the outcome of their case (to either be released or go on to prison), so Choice *D* is not correct.

23. A: Probation and parole are mostly distinguished by when they can be granted and served; probation is possible before incarceration and parole a possibility after serving some time incarcerated. Choice *B* has these reversed, so it is not correct. Parole is what is considered by a parole board, while probation can be granted by a judge, so Choice *C* is incorrect. As noted, the time which each can be served is considered the biggest difference between the two, so Choice *D* is not correct.

24. A: Inmates may have more than one charge against them and depending on their sentence, they can serve those sentences either concurrently or consecutively. With concurrent sentences, inmates can serve both sentences simultaneously, thereby reducing their time of incarceration. If the sentences are served consecutively, then one of the sentences must be completed before the next begins, which results in a longer incarceration.

25. B: Inmate classification is the system whereby inmates are categorized for like placement. They are separated by gender, then age, and whether they are sentenced, detained, or on trial. Of those subsets, they will be classified with a numerical score based upon criteria of charge, history, escape risk probability, and other criteria. The higher the score, the higher their resultant classification and housing unit. The lower the score, the less likely they are to be violent or problematic to the facility. Race is not a factor that is considered in inmate classification.

Legal Definitions and Policies Pertaining to Correctional Facilities

Constitutional Rights of Inmates

Detainee inmates are assumed innocent until proven guilty but they still may lose constitutional rights. While detainee prisoners are entitled to the constitutional rights afforded to ordinary citizens, there are exceptions where such rights are overruled by the correctional facility's need to maintain a safe and secure environment. These exceptions are the right to liberty, the right against search and seizure, and the right to privacy. In correctional settings, the safety and security of the facility are paramount and the need for safety will, at times, overrule constitutional rights, especially in emergency situations.

Sentenced prisoners, on the other hand, are convicted and are stripped of some constitutional rights, such as the right to vote. All prisoners are afforded protection by the Eighth Amendment, which protects against cruel and unusual punishment, and the Fourteenth Amendment, which protects against discriminatory treatment.

The First Amendment

The First Amendment provides for freedom of speech, freedom of religion, and freedom of public assembly. Correctional facilities exercise these freedoms to the extent that good security will permit, but First Amendment rights are limited for the safety and order of the institution. If inmates were permitted to assemble at will and practice religion whenever they wanted, it could create chaos in the correctional facility. Therefore, inmates are permitted to exercise these freedoms, but at times and intervals that still permit the facility to maintain safety and order.

Inmates' Mail
Correctional facilities encourage inmates to communicate with family and friends to help stabilize their behavior inside prison. Communication can take place through the inmate telephone, the United States Postal Service, inmate visits, and even email communication. An inmate's mail and communication may be restricted by court order if he or she has a history of threatening witnesses or communicating with the outside in a manner that presents a clear and present danger to others.

Most inmates can communicate freely with the outside world. Their correspondence is classified as non-legal mail or legal mail, which may be from an attorney or court. Many inmates work on appealing their case or defending other charges while in prison, and may communicate with their attorneys to do so. Inmates who are indigent are provided free attorney calls and free postage for communication with their attorneys. Communication between inmates and their attorneys of record is protected by attorney-client privileges. Correctional staff searching incoming mail may open the mail in the presence of the recipient inmate, as long as they are comfortable that it doesn't contain contraband. Once the mail is deemed safe, it must be given to the inmate without being read.

Regular mail, on the other hand, is subject to vigorous inspection for contraband. Many attempts are made to smuggle contraband into prison facilities through the United States Postal Service. Staff, therefore, must search incoming mail and packages for contraband, which can be embedded in sophisticated ways. Inmates may receive currency or checks in the mail, which can be deposited into their commissary accounts for future spending.

Inmates' Religious Beliefs

Inmates are granted the right to practice their religion, within reason, as protected by the First Amendment. This protection also includes access to meals consistent with religious beliefs. For example, Jewish inmates can elect to be served Kosher meals while Muslim inmates may elect to consume Halal meals.

Clergy are assigned to the facility on a volunteer or paid basis. Inmates can participate in religious services for any universally-recognized religion. If a religion is not universally recognized, but more than one inmate desires to participate in that religion, then the correctional agency will consider permission for the inmates to participate. The facility's programs office coordinates religious services at regular intervals consistent with the practice of the respective inmate's faith. If having all inmates meeting at the service presents a security concern, then inmates in protective custody, or other security-sensitive designations, may receive private delivery of the services.

Inmates' Access to the Media

Correction agencies maintain policies regarding inmate interviews with the media. In some cases, approval must be granted by the agency's central office, and in other cases, the facility's warden can approve the interview. The safety and security of the facility, the impact the interview will have on normal operations, the classification and security level of the inmate, and any other possible issues the interview may present for the agency are considered when determining if the interview will be permitted. Cameras are generally prohibited inside correctional institutions, so if the interview is camera-based as opposed to a verbal interview for print media, it will receive greater scrutiny and the camera may be prohibited.

Inmate Visitation

The First Amendment grants inmates the right to association; visits are also encouraged by the correctional facility to increase stability in the inmate's life. Visits, however, do have restrictions and can have limits imposed such as non-contact visits only, limited duration visits, or allowing only a limited number of visitors. Visitors must be approved by the inmate. This reduces security concerns of fights or otherwise aggravating the inmate. Inmates in restrictive housing or punitive segregation may be denied visitors or may have visitors at a different time than those for general population inmates. An attorney of record is also permitted special visitation hours, called *legal visits,* to meet with their inmate clients to assist with case defense.

Inmates' Access to Books, Newspapers, and Magazines

Inmates are provided access to publications through the right to printed media afforded by the First Amendment. The facility's programs office also strives to keep the inmates' time occupied, and therefore, often provides a book program, newspaper delivery in the inmates' housing unit, and possible access to law library to do casework. The correctional facility will first review the requested material and remove any security-sensitive articles or pornography before permitting the inmate to read it. Inmates in special housing or punitive segregation may have these rights restricted. To maintain good sanitation and to prevent officers from having too much material to comb through during institutional searches, the number of books that an inmate may maintain may be limited.

The Fourth Amendment

The Fourth Amendment provides protection against unreasonable search and seizure. The criteria cited in the Fourth Amendment protections are the need for justification of the search, reasonableness of the subject, and the person's reasonable expectation of privacy.

Reasonableness
The criteria for "reasonable" inside a correctional facility is different than for persons in the general public, because the safety and security of the facility take precedence, so the inmates' rights to privacy is limited inside a correctional facility. Searches must be conducted frequently inside correctional facilities to detect contraband. There are some additional regulations and protections for detainee inmates who are charged with a misdemeanor; they may still be searched will not undergo a strip search. The most extensive type of search is a body cavity search. These searches require the inmate's consent, except in extreme cases when staff members have a reason to believe an inmate is hiding contraband in a body cavity and the search is justified. A body cavity search is usually conducted by a physician, if the situation permits.

Searches
The courts recognize that the need for safety and security in the correctional setting outweigh the protections afforded to the inmate by the Fourth Amendment, and therefore, the courts allow certain types of searches of inmates for lawful purposes.

Inmates are usually searched when entering and leaving the facility and housing unit. They are also searched inside the housing unit, during prescheduled or random searches. Inmates can also be searched pursuant to a security-related incident. Their property can also be searched; searches for contraband are a frequent part of life in a correctional facility. Searches should have a sound basis and reasonable justification to balance the security needs of the facility with the respect for inmates' privacy. When possible, the search should be the least intrusive and provide as much privacy as possible.

Cross-Gender Searches
Searches, when possible, are conducted by staff who are of the same gender as the inmate. In accordance with religious practices, male Muslim inmates are excluded from a search by a female, except in emergency situations when male staff members are unavailable. Strip searches are conducted by staff of the same gender, except in an emergency situation where staff of the same sex are unavailable.

Visual Searches
The least intrusive search is a visual search. A visual search can be performed by staff of either gender, provided the inmate is clothed. If the inmate is unclothed or partially clothed, then guidelines on gender observations may be dictated by the custody level of the inmate and the availability of staff of the same gender. A visual inspection looks for signs of concern such as unusual bulges, outlines of objects, overt injuries, or even signs of substance abuse. If anything suspicious is noted during the visual search, then the officer may be compelled to advance to a pat-down or strip search to determine the cause of the suspicion.

Pat-Down Searches
Pat-down searches of inmates are conducted frequently, particularly when inmates enter and exit housing units or service areas and walk in corridors. In this type of search, the inmate is fully clothed and

faces a wall with his or her feet spread shoulder-width, while the officer runs his or her hands over the outline of the inmate's body, pockets, and groin area to determine if the inmate is concealing any contraband. The officer may also have inmates open their mouths and stick out their tongues. Officers may run their fingers through the inmate's hair to ensure contraband is not hidden in these areas.

Strip or Body Cavity Searches

Strip searches are conducted by staff of the same gender, except in emergencies, when no staff members of the same gender are available. The inmate must remove all clothing and stand in front of the officer and perform a squat to see if anything falls out of the rectum while his or her clothes are searched. During a strip search, the officer cannot perform a cavity search or look into the inmate's rectum. If the officer believes that the inmate is hiding contraband in their rectum, then they must call a supervisor, who will then confirm or negate the suspicion, and when necessary, document the basis for a body cavity search. This body cavity search is usually performed by a clinician in a private setting. Because contraband can be hidden effectively deeper in the body, and therefore pass a shallow cavity search undetected, x-rays may also be used.

With an increasing number of female staff members entering the correctional field, it is not unusual for female officers to be assigned to male facilities and work in close contact with male inmates. The duties of female officers include tours or inspection of areas that contain male inmates and entering areas where privacy can be a concern. However, male officers are restricted from performing these same functions in female facilities, due to the greater privacy needs for the female inmate population.

The Fifth Amendment

The Fifth Amendment to the U.S. Constitution states:

No person shall be held to answer for a capital, or otherwise infamous crime, unless on a presentment or indictment of a grand jury, except in cases arising in the land or naval forces, or in the militia, when in actual service in time of war or public danger; nor shall any person be subject for the same offense to be twice put in jeopardy of life or limb; nor shall be compelled in any criminal case to be a witness against himself, nor be deprived of life, liberty, or property, without due process of law; nor shall private property be taken for public use, without just compensation.

In a criminal setting this simply means that a person cannot be forced to testify against themselves and cannot be tried for the same crime twice in the same jurisdiction. It also provides for due process, meaning that a person cannot be arbitrarily convicted and that administrative procedures that provide notice and an opportunity for defense must be followed.

In a correctional setting, an inmate may receive an institutional infraction for violating a rule or policy. Due process provides for a hearing for which the inmate is permitted time to hear evidence against them, and to prepare a defense and offer witnesses in support of that defense. Under inmates' Fifth Amendment rights, they do not have to speak and can refuse to incriminate themselves.

Treatment Programs

In many cases, rehabilitation is a goal of incarceration. Correctional facilities offer multiple treatment options for offenders. Participation in treatment programs can be mandated by the facility, with the goal of maintaining good institutional behavior. In other cases, it may be an incentive for either early release or for consideration for parole. Inmates can also be awarded less restrictive security housing as a benefit of participating in a treatment program. There are many treatment programs that can be offered that relate to the inmate's criminal charge, such as substance treatment programs, sex offender programs, and behavioral programs, among others.

Inmates may oppose being placed in a treatment program because it could be construed as an admission of guilt for those who pleaded innocent to their criminal charges. Inmates can opt out of programming or be taken out involuntarily, but this will usually affect their classification and may also force a change in their housing assignment.

Miranda Warnings

Miranda warnings are a result of a landmark 1966 Supreme Court case in which a defendant sued the state of Arizona alleging that the police did not inform him that any statement he made could be used against him in court. The Supreme Court ruled that suspects in criminal prosecution must be informed of their rights of due process and self-incrimination before questioning.

In many situations in jails and prisons, Miranda warnings do not apply. Miranda warnings are only required in criminal investigations and not correctional administrative procedures, such as inmate discipline. If the investigation of the inmate is criminal in nature and they are a subject of criminal investigation, then Miranda warnings need to be read to the inmate before interrogation.

The Sixth Amendment

The Sixth Amendment guarantees the rights of criminal defendants, including the right to a speedy public trial, the right to an attorney, a jury of their peers, the right to know the charges, and to challenge evidence and accusers.

Access
In criminal proceedings, defendants must be provided free legal representation if they cannot afford it themselves. In administrative proceedings, inside a jail or prison, inmates must have access to a law library to defend their case. For administrative hearings, they also are permitted guidance, with provisions for an interpreter, if needed.

Privacy
Inmates have the right to privileged communications with their attorney of record. This protects the defendant's right to self-incrimination. Staff may inspect mail from an attorney to the extent of looking for obvious contraband, but must not read the legal mail. Staff cannot listen to privileged calls between an inmate and his or her attorney of record.

Effective Assistance
The inmate must have reasonable attorney access. This does not mean an attorney can visit or call the institution at any time, but it does mean that the facility must schedule time for attorneys to visit and time for inmates to contact attorneys that is reasonable for effective communication. If the inmate cannot afford to call their attorney, then the call will be provided at no cost.

The Eighth Amendment

The Eighth Amendment protects against cruel and unusual punishment. In correctional settings, this can translate into conditions of confinement. Many courts have received petitions from inmates, and as a result, have ruled that minimum standards of care, custody, and control of inmates must be maintained.

Those protections can regulate meals, environmental conditions, access to recreation and services, and even noise and lighting levels. It is not unusual for correctional institutions to be placed under consent decrees or even federal monitoring to make sure the inmates receive a certain standard of care.

Many inmates still petition the courts against cruel and unusual punishment, which can be subjective in certain cases. Some of the typical cruel and unusual punishment complaints involve overcrowding issues, restrictive housing complaints, and limited access to services. Inmates placed in punitive segregation or isolated mental health housing argue that the lack of human contact constitutes cruel and unusual punishment. Inmates who are placed in situations with overcrowding argue that the limited space and long wait for services constitutes cruel and unusual punishment. The courts are arbitrary in their determination of what constitutes cruel and unusual punishment, and it often follows the mood or the political direction of the state or courts of jurisdiction.

Excessive Force

In order to maintain control in correctional setting, the use of force is authorized under federal, state, and local statutes as guided by correctional law and state-specific use of force guidelines. The use of force will escalate according to a use of force continuum, in which, if a lower level of force is not effective to obtain compliance, then the next degree of force may be used. This continuum applies to non-lethal force; deadly physical force can only be used to protect the life of oneself or another or to prevent a violent felony with a potential for serious injuries. A review of the force will take place internally or externally, which will either find that the force was justified and proper, or unjustified. When determined to be unjustified, the inflicting staff member may be subject to administrative sanctions or even criminal charges. Force must cease when the inmate's resistance ceases; otherwise, it will be deemed excessive.

Justified

In order for the force to be justified, it must have followed the use of force policy and continuum. The force must also be deemed lawful and necessary to affect control over the inmate or to prevent injury or harm to others.

Proportionate

The level of force employed should be proportionate to the threat. For example, an inmate who is refusing to go to court and is ordered by the court to do so should not be the subject of punches. The inmate should be carried and no further force should be used if merely carrying the inmate can accomplish the task of getting them on the bus for court. Any injuries to the inmate should be reasonable to the amount of force that staff employed.

To determine if force was excessive, supervisors and oversight agencies will review use of force reports, medical reports, video evidence, photos, and interviews of the involved parties and witnesses to verify that the use of force was both lawful and consistent with the level of threat or resistance. If force is found to be unreasonable, unjustified, or excessive, then the correctional staff can face both administrative and criminal charges. Force should be employed as a last resort, when verbal orders have failed. If the use of force is anticipated, then the correctional staff should notify medical staff to determine if the use of force would be catastrophic to the inmate and to stand by for a medical response. In anticipated force situations, correctional staff should also bring a handheld camera to the scene to record the event.

Liability

Correctional staff can be held accountable for personal liability or vicarious liability. If the corrections officer's actions are deemed unlawful, the agency can choose not to indemnify the staff member, and he or she may be held personally liable for their actions.

Personal Liability

Correctional staff members take an oath to abide by rules and regulations and to provide a defined standard of care to inmates under their charge. If they use excessive force, deny medical treatment to inmates, or deny lawful services that are detrimental to the inmate, then the staff member can be held personally liable.

Vicarious Liability

Correctional staff can also be held liable for failing to stop or report illegal actions of others. They can also be held vicariously liable for omissions from reports and or for denying knowledge of an event they witnessed.

Failure to Protect an Inmate from Another Inmate

Correctional staff members, regardless of their own personal beliefs, have an obligation to keep all inmates safe. There are many ways an officer might neglect their duties:

- Substantial Risk of Harm: If a correctional staff member knowingly places the inmate in a situation with a risk of serious harm, the staff member can be held personally responsible.

- Officer Knew of the Risk: If the officer has specific information that the inmate will likely be injured, then staff can also be held personally liable.

- Unreasonable Failure to Respond: If the officer does not take the appropriate action to keep the inmate safe, then he or she can also be held personally responsible.

- Causation: If the officer's actions, or lack thereof, has a direct relationship to the harm brought upon the inmate, then the officer can be held personally responsible.

Failure-to-Protect Claims

One of the challenges for correctional staff in a jail or prison is to keep prisoners safe from one other. Some of the contributory factors of jail violence include:

- Vulnerable inmates: Corrections staff should identify and isolate inmates who are likely to become a target based upon their charge, physical appearance, or other endangering factors.

- Dangerous inmates: Correction staff should identify predatory inmates and isolate them from the general population inmates.

- Separation: If correctional staff members are aware that an inmate could be a victim of violence or is being extorted by other inmates, then the inmate should be separated from the aggressors.

- Failure to take action: If correctional staff members witness an imminent assault or an assault in progress, they are required to take action to protect the inmate.

- Understaffing: If the correctional administrator maintains a poor staff-to-inmate ratio, it can lead to poor supervision and inmate assaults, for which the administrator can be held responsible.

- Overcrowding: If the facility is holding more inmates than it was designed to house, overcrowding can contribute to inmate violence.

Deliberate Indifference

All inmates have a right to competent medical and mental healthcare. This is a constant challenge for correctional facilities to provide, as inmates arrive in poor mental and physical health. As a result, an inmate's health may deteriorate in prison. Inmate healthcare is frequently challenged by lawsuits, high profile media coverage of poor clinical encounters, and frequent scrutiny by oversight agencies. When an inmate is denied medical or mental healthcare, or is provided poor quality service, they can claim that their Eight Amendment rights have been violated. Correctional staff have an obligation to provide access for inmates to clinical services; neglecting this duty can not only result in administrative discipline, but can lead to criminal charges and civil liability for both the correctional agency and the corrections officials involved.

Actual Knowledge
In order to be held responsible, the corrections official had to have knowledge of the condition or ailment through a reasonable detection or surveillance process.

Failure to act
If a custodial or clinical official had knowledge of a condition requiring care and did not provide that care or access to it, then the official can be held administratively, criminally, and civilly liable.

The Fourteenth Amendment

The Fourteenth Amendment to the Constitution provides a citizen with rights to equal protection of life, liberty, property, and due process of law. This is the most frequently litigated amendment because it protects the rights of citizens, which are often violated. In correctional settings, due process is important because it provides rights and protection to the inmate against being arbitrarily sanctioned.

Due process for inmate infractions follows a schedule, to permit the inmate to present a reasonable defense, as follows:

- The inmate receives a copy of the institutional rules and regulations upon admission to the facility.

- If the inmate violates the rules and regulations, they are served written notice of the violation accusation along with the date, time, and location of the violation.

- The inmate is then provided 24 to 48 hours to prepare a defense, access to free counsel if needed, and access to a law library for defense materials.

- The inmate is then brought to an impartial hearing where they can listen to evidence and question witnesses, while presenting their own witnesses, if necessary.

- The inmate is then given a disposition, and if they do not agree with the disposition, they may appeal the decision within a reasonable timeframe.

- Nothing in this process prevents the facility from changing the classification and moving the inmate to a safer housing unit (pending the outcome of the hearing), for the overall safety and security of the facility.

- Hearings can result in loss of good time or privileges, and transfer to more restrictive punitive segregation housing.

Procedural Due Process Versus Substantive Due Process

Procedural due process is the process in which the discipline or sanction is processed in sequential order. Substantive due process is a challenge to the sanction itself. For example, starving a prisoner for a legitimate infraction would be a violation of substantive due process. In general, due process is the opportunity for inmate to properly defend themselves with reasonable safeguards in any discipline process. This includes the means and opportunity to prepare a defense, question witnesses, and even appeal a finding of guilt.

The Religious Land Use and Institutionalized Persons Act (RLUIPA)

Passed by the United States House of Representatives and the Senate in 2000, the RLUIPA further defines religious freedom of expression. There are two main aspects of the legislation: the first is applicable to religious land use and the second defines religious freedom for prisoners. In essence, this act states that an inmate may exercise their religious rights unless it presents a burden to government interests, and that inmates are free to practice their religion, regardless as to whether it is universally recognized or not. A further Supreme Court ruling on the RLUIPA states that, if the exercise of the inmate's religious beliefs provides a benefit to one inmate over another, it is still lawful for the benefitting inmate to practice that religion while incarcerated.

The *Turner* Test

The *Turner* test is a standard developed as a result of a 1987 court decision in which a prisoner sued an Ohio prison for arbitrary regulations that he felt violated his First Amendment rights. The test is now used as a standard and has four components:

1. To establish if there is a legitimate rationale for the regulation in the interest of security and the good order of the institution.

2. Whether the inmate has a reasonable alternative to exercise the same rights

3. To determine if providing the same rights to all prisoners universally would have a negative impact on the good order of the correctional facility.

4. Whether there is another method to permit the inmate's right without significant cost to the correctional facility.

In essence, to pass the Turner test, the prohibition of an inmate's ability to exercise his or her rights must have sound rationale and a reasonable correctional security need.

A Son of Sam Law

The "Son of Sam" was a nickname given to a serial killer named David Berkowitz, who terrorized New York City in the 1970's. Because his killings were widely publicized, he was given a great deal of notoriety, which he seemed to enjoy. As a result of the notoriety, legislators wanted to ensure he did not profit from his new-found fame. Consequently, the Son of Sam law was passed, which prevents criminals from profiting from their crimes. Subsequently, many other states adopted similar legislation. With current legislative trends working in support of prisoners, the Supreme Court ruled the Son of Sam law was too broad and unduly restricted an inmate's rights to free speech, commencing a trend against mandatory forfeiture of royalties for prisoners.

Prison Rape Elimination Commission

In 2003, because of the growing concern of systemic sexual abuse in jails and prison, Congress passed the Prison Rape Elimination Act (PREA) and created the Prison Rape Elimination Commission. The main focus of the legislation is to "provide for the analysis of the incidence and effects of prison rape in federal, state, and local institutions and to provide information, resources, recommendations, and funding to protect individuals from prison rape."

The impact on correctional facilities is that they are mandated to schedule yearly independent PREA audits, conducted by trained and certified auditors, who will look for signs of abuse and proper reporting, while collecting statistics to analyze and share on a national level. This audit consists of a review of records and documents and private interviews to determine the level of sexual activity in the correctional facility.

Right to Medical Care

Access to medical care for inmates is federally mandated. While incarcerated, inmates obviously are not free to seek their own medical care, so adequate medical care must be provided for them. Inmates are entitled to free medical care for emergencies but may be charged reasonable copayments for sick calls or other routine services. Inmates are also provided dental care, but only to accommodate medical necessity, and cosmetic treatments are not covered.

Many prisoners enter the facility with a host of medical issues that must be triaged and treated. Newly-admitted inmates go through a battery of tests to screen for communicable diseases and to diagnose and treat physical and mental health issues. Medications can be prescribed and are ingested in the presence of staff, to ensure they are consumed by the intended inmate. Medications must be provided without cost. Most medications cannot be given to the inmates to take on their own; inmates must go to a medication window or station where a pharmacist dispenses the prescribed medications or the inmate enters a code to release the medication from a preloaded machine.

Medical Care Claims

Inmates can challenge the quality of their care, either administratively, or in many cases, through civil litigation. The basis for the complaint may take the form of a denial or delay of care. The inmate should have access to speedy medical treatment for acute illnesses. Routine requests for treatment of colds or rashes can be accommodated during daily sick call or clinical rounds to the housing unit. Any immediate care need, such as an asthma attack, must be met with a medical response team or immediate escort to the clinic. Failure to do so can result in liability against the facility and the correctional staff member.

Many correctional institutions outsource medical and mental healthcare services to private medical and mental health providers. All correctional facilities try to reduce healthcare costs through telemedicine, urgent care centers to reduce inmate hospital runs and electronic medical records. Many inmates are repeat offenders, and if clinicians have the inmate's medical history on file from a previous incarceration, it helps reduce duplicative testing on that inmate, which will reduce medical costs.

Medical Care Lawsuits

Current focus on correctional healthcare trends suggests poor medical and mental health treatment outcomes for inmates. For medical and mental health practitioners, correctional facilities provide unique challenges. Inmates usually enter the facility in a deteriorated physical and mental health state, after having no form of routine care on the outside. Inmates, in general, have a host of medical and mental health issues related to dependency. In many instances, inmate healthcare is outsourced to private for-profit vendors, who may take shortcuts to preserve profits. Inmates can easily initiate lawsuits through their access to law libraries, where they can initiate their own litigation against medical and mental health treatment at little or no cost. As a result, inmate lawsuits against medical care are common.

HIV and AIDS

HIV is the acronym for Human Immunodeficiency Virus, while AIDS is the acronym for Acquired Immunodeficiency Syndrome. The difference between the two is that HIV is the actual virus and AIDS is the resulting condition caused by the virus. The virus is spread through bodily fluids such as blood, semen, and breast milk. Unlike tuberculosis, it is not airborne and cannot be spread through casual contact. It is most commonly spread through unprotected sex and the sharing of syringes. The prevalence is higher in inmate populations than in the general public. In correctional settings, inmates with HIV are usually isolated in a hospital or infirmary-type setting for disease surveillance and for the ease of treatment by medical practitioners.

Sexually Transmitted Diseases (STDs)

Because sexually transmitted diseases are spread through unprotected sex and the use of intravenous needles, the inmate population is more susceptible to STDs then the general public. While it is against correctional policy, inmates may still engage in consensual sex. Some correctional agencies recognize this and provide condoms to inmates upon request to prevent the spread of sexually transmitted diseases. The most common sexually transmitted diseases are syphilis, gonorrhea, chlamydia, and herpes. Part of inmate orientation educates inmates on the health concerns associated with sexually transmitted diseases.

Tuberculosis

Tuberculosis is a disease of the lungs, throat, spine, and brain that is associated with chronic coughing, chills, fevers, and large amounts of sputum. Because a goal of the correctional agency is to prevent the spread of communicable disease, new admission inmates are given a TB test upon admission to the facility and then incubated with other similarly-tested inmates until they clear the incubation period. The inmate is given a skin test that results in a red ring on their forearm if positive. Even if the test reveals positive results, it can be a false positive result, and a chest x-ray is needed next to rule out TB. If the inmate is identified positive for TB, they will be isolated from the rest of the inmates to begin their treatment plan. The inmate may even be placed in a negative pressure cell, which imports and exports air from outside the facility, so as not to spread the disease through the internal HVAC system. Staff receive special training to manage TB inmate populations. The spread of the disease is generally through prolonged airborne contact.

Diabetes

Because many inmates practice poor diet and exercise rituals, they are at a higher risk for diabetes. Diabetes is the inability of the body to produce or effectively use insulin, so the inmate has to regulate and supplement their insulin. If the inmate utilized an insulin pump while on the outside, the facility may choose to prohibit the inmate from keeping that pump in the facility, and may instead elect to dispense the insulin from the clinic. Diabetic inmates are also given a special diet and their health is monitored more closely then general population inmates.

Epilepsy

Epilepsy is common among prisoners and is identified as a seizure disorder, caused by sporadic electrical activity in the brain. Inmates with a history of seizures may be prescribed anti-seizure medication. Staff are trained how to treat inmates experiencing seizures, which is to immediately notify a medical response team, remove anything dangerous from the immediate area that could harm the inmate, and to monitor the inmate for further deterioration until a medical team arrives.

Disability and the ADA

Disabled inmates are entitled to the same protections and rights that they would receive if not incarcerated. This means providing accommodations for wheelchair access, sign language interpreters if needed, and any other reasonable accommodation to assist their disability. Correctional staff must treat an inmate with a disability without prejudice. The disabled inmate may be entitled to a reasonable accommodation, such as wheelchair-bound inmates being housed as close to services as possible to avoid extensive transport in a wheelchair. Facility emergency response devices, such as fire alarms, must not only have sounds to accommodate blind inmates, but must also have strobe lights to accommodate deaf inmates. The facility must take every reasonable step to accommodate inmates with disabilities to the extent it does not compromise the safety and security of the facility.

Pregnant Inmates

Some female prisoners may be incarcerated while pregnant. The facility will be required to provide prenatal care and education. Part of the prenatal care is to provide access to elective abortion if desired by the inmate up to the term limits permitted by law. If the mother delivers the baby to term, some institutions will permit the mother to keep the baby at the facility, provided the facility has a nursery program and that certain criteria of the mother are met. For example, she must have a non-violent criminal history and successfully pass of a mental health screen. If the mother is permitted to maintain the baby in the nursery, it will only be for a short time. Female prisoners generally have more medical issues than male prisoners, because female prisoners have a greater prevalence of drug dependency issues.

Suicide

Inmate suicide is a major concern of most correctional administrators. Inmates are at a high risk for suicide, driven by the trauma of first-time arrests, stress from embarrassment, feelings of failure, and issues related to the withdrawal of drugs and alcohol. Therefore, correctional administrators try to identify "at risk" inmates and provide tools and enhanced observation to reduce the possibility of suicide. Some of those tools are good screening for inmates who may show a higher risk of suicide, such as first-time offenders, inmates having a heinous criminal charge, or other unusual behavior. Newly admitted inmates receive screening by medical and mental health professionals, who look for warning signs of suicidal behavior. Newly admitted inmates are generally placed in a dormitory-type environment if their classification permits, which allows for better surveillance of mental health issues by staff and other inmates. In new admission housing units, the facility may also employ suicide aides, who are inmate workers paid to patrol the area to look for signs of inmate suicide, in order to supplement the officers' efforts to prevent suicides. Inmates deemed to have mental health concerns are housed in mental health units, which provide a greater staff-to-inmate ratio, and provide greater access to specialized clinical staff in a dormitory-type setting. The inmate's shoelaces and belt are taken to prevent self-strangulation and the area is modified to eliminate the potential for suicide. For example, shower nozzles are flush with the wall to prevent an inmate from tying a ligature to it.

Viral Hepatitis

Viral hepatitis is a disease that affects people in many ways and can cause fatigue, loss of appetite, and other symptoms. It is spread through either oral contact with feces or through blood-to-blood exposure. While it is rare that an inmate may develop hepatitis while incarcerated, some do enter the facility with hepatitis after leading a poor quality of life on the outside. Most strains of hepatitis are treatable, but Hepatitis C can ultimately be fatal.

Asthma

Asthma is a disease of the lungs that causes shortness of breath and can lead to death. Inmates who have asthma may be permitted to keep a medical rescue inhaler for acute bouts of asthma. If provided to the inmate, it will be through a prescription after being diagnosed by a clinician through a clinical encounter. Any inmates coming in with their own medication must be assessed by medical staff to evaluate if the prescription should be continued. Inmates with asthma may be provided a smoke-free environment, provided the facility is not already smoke-free.

Drug abuse

Most inmates are incarcerated for drug-related offenses and a good portion of inmates have a history of substance abuse. A newly admitted inmate who enters as an addict may be prescribed methadone, which is a synthetic drug used to wean an individual off real drugs. While it may be difficult to comprehend, many inmates still engage in drug use behind bars, utilizing contraband drugs sold in the prison black market. To combat this, inmates are given drug screening tests inside the prison and positive results can result in loss of good time or privileges, or other sanctions. Contraband drugs are often intercepted in the mail, visit area, or in the housing units during searches.

Personality Disorders

A personality disorder is mental deviation from expected norms and behaviors. These deviations can be related to personal, social, and occupational norms. Some personality disorders are mild, while others are severe. More severe behaviors may need medication to manage. Personality disorders can manifest into dramatic, erratic, and antisocial behaviors, among other deviations. In correctional settings, administrators try to manage personality disorders so they do not impact the good order of the facility.

Schizophrenia

Schizophrenia is a personality disorder associated with delusional thoughts, hallucinations, and withdrawn behavior. Recognition and treatment in a correctional setting is important because if the schizophrenia is left unmanaged, it can lead to problems with other prisoners and possibly bring harm to staff. Psychotic disorders are characterized by disorganized thoughts, hallucinations, and impaired psychosocial skills.

Mental Health Treatment

It is not unusual for a significant portion of any correctional population to be on psychotropic medications of some form. Correctional facilities will triage and diagnose newly admitted inmates and follow up with aftercare. Any inmates deemed to have mental health problems may be prescribed medications to control their illness. Some acute mental health cases may go the mental health housing units or assigned to a one-on-one watch, while others may be prescribed medication while still being permitted to remain in general population. The goal is to manage behaviors so inmates are not self-injurious, injurious to other inmates or staff, and do not present a security danger to the facility. Inmate medication may be force-fed to control inmate behavior, after exhausting all alternatives, and if used at minimal levels. Inmates may also be assigned to a one-on-one watch with a one officer per inmate ratio. This type of supervision is expensive but may be needed when an extremely unstable inmate is exhibiting suicidal tendencies.

Elderly and Terminally-Ill Inmates

Young, strong, robust inmates are often depicted in prison movies, but the reality is that America's prison population is aging. The aging population requires extensive medical treatment and accommodations for illnesses that are prevalent in the elderly. Even inmates with terminal illnesses need to be treated, and it is rare that an inmate will be granted a compassionate discharge. Inmate health aides are trained to provide hospice to terminal inmates, and correctional agencies designate areas for acute medical treatment to treat their aging populations.

Dental Care

As part of constitutionally-mandated medical care, inmates are provided access to a dentist. The dental care is not for preventative or cosmetic treatment, but for acute dental issues such as cavities, root canals, and dental pain management issues. Inmates are also provided free dental hygiene items, such as a toothbrush and toothpaste. Dentists usually practice in the facility on a part-time basis and appointments must be set for the inmate in advance. The inmate population is at a high risk for dental problems.

Bloodborne Pathogens (BBP) Programs

It is in the best interest of the facility to prevent the spread of disease through bloodborne pathogens. All correctional staff are provided training on the reasonable steps and universal precautions to avoid exposure. When permitted, staff are provided gloves, masks, and protective clothing to limit the exposure to blood and bodily fluids. Sanitarians train inmate environmental teams in the cleanup of blood and fluids to help limit the risk of exposure to bloodborne pathogens. Staff are also encouraged to get vaccinations to protect themselves against hepatitis B, and universal precautions must be taught, employed, and posted to limit contamination.

Fee-for-Service Programs

Constitutionally inferred rights provide for access to medical care for inmates and especially indigent populations. This includes assessment, triage, emergency response, and aftercare. While medical treatment must be provided regardless of the inmate's financial status, some facilities may impose a copay to limit frivolous clinical encounters for inmates who may have chronic unsubstantiated medical complaints or those who just want to travel to the clinic for sick call to get out of their housing unit for a little while. The facility may impose a nominal surcharge, such as $2, which may seem minor, but is significant to an inmate with limited funds, and may help prevent an unnecessary clinical encounter.

In any event, these surcharge fees should not impede or delay medical treatment as requested by the inmate in any way; otherwise, the facility or correctional staff member can be held liable.

Civil Rights Law Suits

Federal civil right protections extend to all persons, including inmates. Civil rights of prisoners are constantly the subject of litigation and federal oversight has been established in jurisdictions where civil rights violations appear systemic. There are two common forms of civil right violations. The first is when the facility or agency has a policy, practice, or procedure that, by design, violates the civil rights of inmates. The second form of violation is when the facility has a policy or procedure that complies with civil right laws, but the correctional staff knowingly violates it. These violations can lead to class action lawsuits, federal oversight, punitive damages and mandated federal monitoring. Staff are trained to offer care, custody, and control of the prisoners and must not deviate from institutional policies.

Courts Play in the Judicial System

Correctional facilities are often the focus of litigation, which can range from complaints about lighting levels to complaints about placement in isolation. Most related court cases involve the interpretation of cruel and unusual punishment, which is often left to broad interpretation. In the use of isolation for example, the facility will likely argue that it keeps other inmates safe, while the subject of the isolation may argue that depravation of human contact has adverse effects on him or her. Court rulings in these matters can be arbitrary and may lead to a policy change if the complaint is upheld. Correctional administrators must form policies that are fair to the inmates but that maintain a safe and secure custodial environment. Correctional facilities are the frequent target of court oversight on a federal, state, and local level, especially in light of recent prison reform movements.

The Supreme Court

The Supreme Court is the highest court in the United States and has handed down landmark decisions that affect the criminal justice system. Historically, the Supreme Court has avoided decisions that directly impacted correctional facilities, but with the advent of high profile prison riots related to poor conditions of confinement that transpired in the 1960's and 1970's, the Supreme Court became more involved in upholding prisoners' civil rights. Lawsuits from prisoners began to flood in, and to reduce frivolous lawsuits, the courts developed the Prison Litigation Reform Act.

The Prison Litigation Reform Act

Because inmates have free access to law libraries in the correctional facilities and because indigent inmates can file law suits at no cost, there was a time that inmates began to file multiple lawsuits, which placed an undue burden on the court system. As a result, the Prison Litigation Reform Act was created in the 1990's to place a reasonable burden on the inmate to ensure a claim they brought forth had merit. It also created limitations for those inmates with a prior history of filing suits that were frivolous.

Inmate Litigation

Inmate litigation usually falls into one of three categories:

> 1. Tort: When an inmate claims to have injury or harm from an action caused by a person, policy, or lack or denial or services. For example, if an inmate claims to have been assaulted by staff, his or her claim will fall under a tort.

> 2. Habeas Corpus: This is when an inmate questions the legitimacy of his or her detention and the correctional agency must prove the legitimacy to the court.

> 3. Civil rights violation: This is when a prisoner claims a federally protected right is violated. One example is if an inmate claims an officer assaulted him because of his race and shouted racial epithets during the alleged assault.

Inmate litigation in the past has resulted in punitive damage awards, policy change, and changes of conditions of confinement. Correctional facilities are inundated with multiple challenges to conditions of confinement.

Agency and the Supervisor Liability

There are different reasons that an agency may be held liable for violations of civil rights. This may occur if a policy or procedure does not afford for preservation of that civil right, or if the procedure to protect the civil right is present, but the staff member does not follow the procedure or denies the inmate the right to that procedure. In the latter case, it is still considered a violation regardless as to whether it was intentional or a resulted from a lack of training.

Supervisors can also be held accountable for failing to remedy a situation that protects inmates' rights or for failing to take action when required. Supervisors are directly responsible for actions of those under their charge.

Access to Courts

Because the criminal justice system recognizes an inmate's right to a defense, the facility must provide access to a well-equipped law library for inmates to research and prepare a defense as they might otherwise be entitled to if not incarcerated. The law library should be equipped with a legal assistant, law books, research materials, and copy machine. Inmates are permitted reasonable access at scheduled times and upon request. If the inmate does not understand the legal process, he or she will be afforded a legal aid representative who will help the inmate navigate the material in the law library. Even inmates in punitive segregation cannot be denied access to law library materials, and if their presence in the law library will present a security challenge, then the material must be brought to them. If an interpreter is needed, one must be provided. Inmates must also be permitted to receive visits from their attorney of record for defense purposes. These visits generally follow a scheduled time for attorney visits.

Types of Discovery

In simple terms, the word *discovery* in formal court proceedings is when each opposing side is asked to supply documents and evidence for the other side to review and defend. This permits each side to learn what the opposing side is presenting and mount a defense, so as not to waste the court's time. It is also a time for either side to request documents or evidence from the opposing side that they feel might assist their case.

Trial Avoidance Techniques

Ninety-five percent or more of criminal cases never make it to the trial stage. Parties are strongly urged to reconcile prior to a trial to avoid the burden and expense of the court system. Some prosecutors offer a plea deal that is less than a sentence might otherwise impose, in order to provide an incentive for the other party to settle the case and avoid a trial. In civil cases, both parties can agree to a *summary judgment*, which essentially asks a judge to rule on an argument in which both sides are in agreement about the main facts of the case. Defendants can also file a motion to dismiss on a technicality or rule of law.

Some good rules for testifying witnesses include:

- Witnesses should prepare with their attorney or representative prior to providing a testimony.

- Witnesses should dress well and arrive early for their testimony.

- Witnesses should only answer the questions asked and should not provide additional information, which may lead the interviewer to another series of questions.

- Witnesses should speak slowly, clearly, and should not use acronyms or correctional jargon that laypersons may not understand.

- Witness should look to their attorney to see if they object to the question before answering.

- Witness should answer truthfully and to the best of their knowledge and not guess or speculate.

Glossary

- Segregation: Inmates may be segregated or separated from each other for safety reasons or to preserve good order in the institution.

- Serious incident: Any event that results in injury or involves imminent injury, or that threatens the safety and security of the institution.

- Severe mental disturbance: Occurs when an inmate who is experiencing a bout or episode of mental instability.

- Shadow board: A shadow board is a board where items are hung and then outlined on the board backing, so that when the item is missing from the board, the shape of the missing item is still outlined on the board.

- Shakedowns: The term for searches of inmates and their property.

- Shivs/shanks: The prison term for homemade weapons.

- Special diets: Special meals are prepared for inmates requiring medically-supervised meals or meals prepared according to religious guidelines.

- Strip search: A type of search where the inmate must remove all articles of clothing, which are searched separately.

- Supermax institutions: Supermax refers to institutions reserved for inmates who pose high security concerns, the propensity for escape, or serving long-term sentences.

- Three-piece suit: Prison jargon for handcuffs, leg irons, and a waist chain that keeps the handcuffs close to the prisoner's waist.

- Training: Education performed for the staff or inmates to help them better understand and perform their duties.

- Type I facility: A facility which houses the lowest custody level of prisoners, also known as minimum security.

- Type II facility: A facility that houses prisoners requiring a middle-level of security, also known as a medium security facility.

- Unit Management: A system of management that provides a steady concentration to supervise a designated unit.

- Unity of command: Also known as chain of command, it refers to when each person reports to the next in a clearly defined hierarchy.

- Universal precautions: Using the same method of contagion precautions for all persons regardless of disease status to limit the spread of disease.

- Urine surveillance program: Also known as drug screening, it is a process in which inmates must submit urine samples at frequent intervals for testing.

- Volunteer: An individual who provides time to assist correctional facility inmate programs without compensation.

- Warden: The term used to describe the head of a correctional facility, who may also be called a superintendent.

- Work release: Some inmates are permitted to leave the facility to attend a verified work opportunity to help them transition to the community upon release with gainful employment.

Practice Questions

1. Which of the following is the most accurate statement regarding constitutional rights as they relate to prisoners?
   a. Prisoners can never lose constitutional rights
   b. Prisoners lose all constitutional rights
   c. Prisoners lose some constitutional rights
   d. Only sentenced prisoners lose constitutional rights

2. The First Amendment provides for which of the following?
   a. Freedom of speech, religion, and public assembly
   b. Protection against illegal search and seizure
   c. Protection from cruel and unusual punishment
   d. Access to due process

3. You are the corrections officer assigned to an inmate housing unit. A letter for an inmate arrives written by that inmate's family member. Which of the following is the best course of action to take based upon what you know about an inmate's right to communication?
   a. Search the mail for obvious contraband but do not read it and if there is no contraband, you can give the mail to the inmate.
   b. The inmate can only receive legal mail after it has been searched and reviewed, and cannot receive personal mail.
   c. The inmate must be given the mail without it being searched.
   d. Search the mail and if after reviewing it, if it does not present a danger to the facility or contain security-sensitive information, then you can give them the mail.

4. Which of the following is true regarding an inmate's access to books, newspapers, magazines, and similar materials?
   a. Inmates are not permitted to have access to these materials.
   b. Inmates can have access to these materials as long as they do not have an amount that presents a sanitation concern or search problem for staff.
   c. An inmate's constitutional rights permit them to have as many books, newspapers, and magazines as they wish.
   d. Only inmates in punitive segregation or isolation can have books, magazines, and similar materials.

5. What is the most intrusive type of inmate search called?
   a. Pat Frisk
   b. Strip search
   c. Body cavity search
   d. Complete search

6. You are a female officer working an inmate housing unit when an inmate with an identification card that lists him as a Muslim needs to be searched. The inmate objects to you searching him and requests a male officer search him, if available. You should do which of the following?

    a. Deny the inmate's request and search him anyway.

    b. Approve the inmate's request if a male officer is present.

    c. Approve the inmate's request only if you were conducting a body cavity search.

    d. Deny the inmate's request because security is more important than religious protection.

7. In a correctional setting, due process is best described as which of the following?

    a. The process where an inmate does not have to incriminate themselves.

    b. The process against illegal search and seizure.

    c. An inmate receiving an infraction for an institutional violation.

    d. The process where the inmate has rights to procedures and steps to prepare an adequate defense when accused.

8. In reference to treatment programs in correctional facilities, which of the following is most accurate?

    a. Inmates are not obligated to participate in treatment programs.

    b. Only inmates with good behavior will be offered treatment programs.

    c. All inmates have access to and are encouraged to participate in treatment programs with some programming mandatory for the inmate to remain in preferred housing units.

    d. Inmates need to participate in treatment programs to obtain an early release.

9. You are an officer investigating an inmate infraction when you question an inmate about violating an institutional rule. The inmate refuses to talk, stating he was never given his Miranda warnings. You should respond by informing the inmate in what way?

    a. Advising the inmate of their Miranda warnings and then question the inmate.

    b. You can never question the inmate until they are informed of their Miranda warnings and have an opportunity to consult with an attorney.

    c. Advise the inmate of their due process then commence the questioning.

    d. Advise the inmate that Miranda warnings are only applicable to criminal investigations.

10. If you are working a housing unit and a letter is delivered to an inmate from their attorney of record, you should do which of the following?

    a. Search the mail as you would any other letter, looking for security-related content, which may be detrimental to the facility.

    b. Search the mail only for obvious contraband and then give the letter to the inmate without reading it.

    c. The law library will deliver the legal mail to the inmate after processing it.

    d. Contact a supervisor for further instructions.

11. Which of the following amendments protects the inmate against cruel and unusual punishment?

    a. The First Amendment

    b. The Eighth Amendment

    c. The Twelfth Amendment

    d. Due process of law protects an inmate against cruel and unusual punishment.

12. When it comes to liability in a correctional setting, what are the two most common forms?
    a. Personal liability and vicarious liability
    b. Personal liability and supervisory liability
    c. Vicarious liability and liability through inaction
    d. Excessive force and personal liability

13. You are working as a corrections officer in an inmate housing unit and see an inmate punch another officer in the face and then walk away. According to proper use of force applications, you should do which of the following?
    a. Strike the inmate only with the same level of force.
    b. You cannot use force because the inmate's action has stopped.
    c. You can use all levels of force except deadly physical force.
    d. You can use all levels of force to include deadly physical force.

14. If a corrections officer denies access to the clinic for an inmate with a legitimate need, which of the following sanctions might the officer face as a result?
    a. They can be held administratively liable.
    b. They can be held administratively and civilly liable.
    c. They can be held administrative, civilly, and criminally liable.
    d. They can be charged under a violation of constitutional rights related to the First Amendment.

15. Which of the following best describes the difference between procedural due process versus substantive due process?
    a. Substantive due process is when the discipline or sanction is processed in sequential order, while procedural due process is a challenge to the sanction itself.
    b. Procedural due process is the process in which the discipline or sanction is processed in a sequential order, while substantive due process is a challenge to the sanction itself.
    c. Procedural due process deals with the process, while substantive deals with the substance of the criminal act.
    d. The only difference between the two is that procedural involves administrative proceedings and substantive involves criminal proceedings.

16. Which Act, passed by the House of Representatives and the Senate in 2000, further defines an inmate's right to freedom of expression?
    a. The Prison Rape Elimination Act (PREA)
    b. The Civil Rights Act
    c. The Son of Sam Act
    d. The Religious Land Use and Institutionalized Persons Act (RLUIPA)

17. In reference to the *Turner* test, which of the following is NOT one of the four standards of the exam?
    a. To establish if there is a legitimate rationale for the regulation, in the interest of security and the good order of the institution.
    b. Whether the inmate has a reasonable alternative to exercise the same rights.
    c. The inmate's right to a speedy trial.
    d. Whether there is another method to permit the inmate's right, without significant cost to the correctional facility.

18. In summary, the Son of Sam law mandates which of the following?

    a. That an inmate shall not profit from publicity of their crimes.

    b. That an inmate shall have the right to due process.

    c. That an inmate shall have the right to a speedy trial.

    d. That a supervisor can be responsible for the actions of officers under their charge.

19. Which of the following is the main impact of the Prison Rape Elimination Act (PREA) on correctional facilities?

    a. They have to schedule yearly audit conducted by trained, independent auditors.

    b. They have to report directly to Congress any instance of sexual abuse.

    c. They have to separate rapists from other prisoners.

    d. The PREA Act has no direct impact on correctional facilities.

20. You are working as a corrections officer in a new admission housing unit when an inmate approaches you and said he has a red ring on his forearm where he was recently tested by the clinic. Based upon your knowledge of communicable diseases, which one of the following conditions is the inmate most likely experiencing?

    a. Diabetes

    b. Schizophrenia

    c. Asthma

    d. Tuberculosis

21. You are a supervisor assigned to a correctional facility when an inmate entering the facility requests a special accommodation for a disability. Which of the following is the best course of action?

    a. Accommodate the inmate's request as long as it is consistent with the security of the facility.

    b. You are required to grant the inmates request, even if it presents a breach to the safety and security of the facility.

    c. You are under no obligation to provide the inmate with any special accommodation so you should treat them as you would any other prisoner.

    d. Inmates do not generally tell the truth, so unless you have a note from his or her doctor, you do not have to honor any special request.

22. Pregnant female inmates may be permitted to keep their babies for a short while upon birth provided they meet which of the following types of criteria?

    a. No actual criteria is considered.

    b. They have completed high school and a certain level of prerequisite courses.

    c. They are a legal adult with the ability to pay for the baby's costs.

    d. They are able to pass a mental health screen and have a non-violent criminal history.

23. Which of the following is the LEAST effective correctional tool against potential suicide?

    a. Taking an inmate's belt and shoelaces.

    b. Placing an inmate on a one-on-one watch.

    c. Watching the inmate through a remote surveillance camera.

    d. A screening upon admission by medical and mental health professionals.

24. Which of the following would methadone be used for?
    a. To wean an inmate off of a drug addiction.
    b. To treat schizophrenia
    c. To treat alcoholism
    d. Methadone is a black-market drug used by inmates in the jail or prison.

25. Which of the following is NOT considered a form of prison litigation?
    a. A tort
    b. Habeas Corpus
    c. Due process
    d. A civil rights violation

Answer Explanations

1. C: Inmates lose constitutional rights upon being institutionalized, including liberty and rights to search and seizure. Sentenced prisoners lose even more constitutional rights, such as the right to vote. The loss of rights is only to the extent the facility needs to maintain safety and security and are not just arbitrarily withheld.

2. A: The First Amendment provides for freedom of speech, freedom of religion, and freedom of public assembly. In a correctional setting, these freedoms are permitted within reasonable limits. The rights mentioned in the other answer choices are protected by other Amendments.

3. D: Inmate mail can be searched for contraband, escape details or material, pornographic material, and other security sensitive information. Attorney mail is protected by law and permits the officer to look for obvious contraband, but they cannot read the content that might compromise the inmate's defense. Choice *C* is incorrect because all mail can be searched. Choice *B* involves an attorney, which doesn't apply to this mail from a family member, and Choice *A* is incorrect because the officer can screen the non-legal mail for security-sensitive information.

4. B: Inmates are permitted to have as many books as they desire, as long as it does not pose a sanitation problem or search problem for staff members. Therefore, since inmates can have books, Choice *A* is incorrect. The limit on books rules out Choice *C,* and inmates in punitive segregation may have books restricted. They certainly don't receive books or magazines more than general population inmates, so Choice *D* is incorrect.

5. C: A body cavity search is the most intrusive type of search because it involves a physician looking in an inmate's body cavity. A pat frisk is not intrusive because no clothes are removed. A strip frisk does infringe upon privacy but not to the extent a cavity search does, so this rules out Choice *C*. Choice *D* is incorrect because a "complete search" is not a type of search.

6. B: This answer is the most correct because, when possible, searches are conducted by staff of the same gender as the inmates, especially as it relates to Muslim inmates. Choice *A* is incorrect because the search can't be denied, Choice *C* is incorrect because the type of search does not matter, and Choice *D* is incorrect because the search must be conducted, and religious protection does not take precedence over the search.

7. D: Due process is the procedure for an inmate to prepare and work through a proper defense. Choice *A* is incorrect because it has nothing to do with self-incrimination. Choice *C* is incorrect because it has nothing to do with a body cavity search, and Choice *B* is incorrect because illegal search and seizure has to do with constitutional rights, not inmate due process.

8. C: Inmates are encouraged to participate in treatment programs and in some cases, it may be mandatory for the inmate to participate to maintain housing. Choice *A* is incorrect because some inmates may, in fact, be obligated to participate in a treatment program. Choice *B* is incorrect because treatment programs are for all inmates, and Choice *D* is incorrect because participation in a treatment program is not an absolute requirement for early release.

9. D: Miranda warnings relate to criminal investigations, not administrative procedures, such as an infraction investigation. Therefore, Choices *A* and *B* are incorrect because Miranda warnings are not necessary, and Choice *C* is incorrect because one can question an inmate without due process because it is an administrative proceeding.

10. B: Inmates are permitted to receive mail from an attorney without it being read after it is inspected for contraband. Choice *A* is incorrect because legal mail cannot be read. Choice *C* is incorrect because the law library does not deliver mail, and Choice *D* is incorrect because the officer has clear guidelines in reference to legal mail that they should follow and should not need to call a supervisor.

11. B: The Eighth Amendment protects against cruel and unusual punishment, which makes all other answers incorrect as these other Amendments provide other rights.

12. A: Correctional staff can be held personally liable for the actions of others through vicarious liability. Choices *B* and *C* are fictitious. Choice *D* is incorrect because excessive force is a situation that can lead to a liability, but it is not a type of liability.

13. B: In applications of use of force, the force must be consistent with the threat. If the inmate stopped his assault or aggression, then the officer cannot use force. If the officer cannot use force, then Choices *A*, *C* and *D* are incorrect.

14. C: Inmates have a right to medical care, and if an officer denies them access to the clinic and the inmate subsequently dies, the officer can be held liable administratively, criminally (if criminal intent was present), or can even be sued civilly, which makes Choices *A* and *B* incorrect. Choice *D* is incorrect because the First amendment does not relate to inmate health care.

15. B: Due process is the opportunity for the inmate to properly defend themselves with reasonable safeguards in any disciplinary process. Procedural due process relates to the actual process, while substantive due process relates to the outcome or basis of the individual steps. If Choice *B* is correct, then Choice *A* is incorrect, as it is the opposite answer. The process has nothing to do with criminality, which makes Choices *C* and *D* also incorrect.

16. D: The RLUIPA further defines religious freedom of expression. Although vaguely related, Choice *C* has more to do with inhibiting expression.

17. C: A speedy trial is a constitutional right and not one of the four components of the Turner test, which makes Choices *A*, *B*, and *D* incorrect as they are three of the four actual components.

18. A: The Son of Sam law prohibits an inmate from profiting from their crime. Choice *B* is incorrect because due process has nothing to do with the Son of Sam law. Choice *C* is incorrect because a speedy trial is a constitutional right and not related to the Son of Sam legislation. Choice *D* is incorrect because it references liability, which is not related to the Son of Sam legislation.

19. A: Facilities are required to get independent audits. Choice *B* is incorrect because although PREA was established by Congress, there is no individual reporting requirement to Congress. Choice *C* is incorrect because there are no requirements for separation of prisoners, and Choice *D* is incorrect because PREA has had a major impact on correctional facilities.

20. D: Tuberculosis tests, if positive, can exhibit a red ring on the forearm after testing.

21. A: Under the ADA, disabled inmates are entitled to reasonable accommodations. Therefore, Choice *B* is incorrect because if the accommodation is outweighed by a security need, then the security need take precedence. Choice *C* is incorrect because the facility is under the regulations of the ADA, and Choice *D* is incorrect because you cannot assume that inmates do not tell the truth.

22. D: Possible criteria include the ability to pass a mental health screen and have a non-violent criminal history. The types of considerations mentioned in the other answer choices are not as relevant to being allowed to spend time with one's infant child, and Choice *A* is incorrect by virtue that there are the stated criteria described in Choice *D* for mothers.

23. C: Watching an inmate on a surveillance camera is the least effective method for preventing suicide. The inmate can hide out of camera range, the officer might have to watch several cameras and thus become distracted, or the officer may miss sounds and smells to help prevent suicide, so watching a monitor is the least effective method. Choices *A*, *B*, and *D* are all effective suicide prevention techniques.

24. A: Methadone is a synthetic drug used to wean inmates off narcotics. The other answer choices are not mentioned in connection with Methadone.

25. C: Due process is an administrative process, not a type of litigation. Choices *A*, *B*, and *D* are all forms of litigation, which makes Choice *C* the only correct answer.

FREE Test Taking Tips DVD Offer

To help us better serve you, we have developed a Test Taking Tips DVD that we would like to give you for FREE. **This DVD covers world-class test taking tips that you can use to be even more successful when you are taking your test.**

All that we ask is that you email us your feedback about your study guide. Please let us know what you thought about it – whether that is good, bad or indifferent.

To get your **FREE Test Taking Tips DVD**, email freedvd@studyguideteam.com with "FREE DVD" in the subject line and the following information in the body of the email:

      a. The title of your study guide.

      b. Your product rating on a scale of 1-5, with 5 being the highest rating.

      c. Your feedback about the study guide. What did you think of it?

      d. Your full name and shipping address to send your free DVD.

If you have any questions or concerns, please don't hesitate to contact us at freedvd@studyguideteam.com.

Thanks again!

CPSIA information can be obtained
at www.ICGtesting.com
Printed in the USA
LVHW10s2251191018
594247LV00007B/42/P